The Apache

Titles in the Indigenous Peoples of North America Series Include:

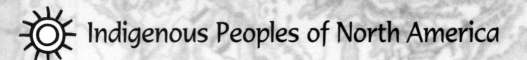
Indigenous Peoples of North America

The Apache

Anne Ake

Lucent Books, Inc.
P.O. Box 289011, San Diego, California

Library of Congress Cataloging-in-Publication Data

Ake, Anne.
    The Apache / by Anne Ake.
        p.   cm. — (Indigenous peoples of North America)
    Includes bibliographical references and index.
    Summary: Discusses the origins, way of life, spirituality, and social
    organization of the Apache nations, as well as their relationships with
    the European settlers.
    ISBN 1-56006-616-4 (hardcover)
    1. Apache Indians—History—Juvenile literature. 2. Apache Indians—
    Social life and Customs—Juvenile literature. [1. Apache Indians. 2.
    Indians of North America—New Mexico.] I. Title. II. Series.
    E99.A6 A57 2001
    979.004'972—dc21

00-008758

Contents

Foreword

North America's native peoples are often relegated to history—viewed primarily as remnants of another era—or cast in the stereotypical images long found in popular entertainment and even literature. Efforts to characterize Native Americans typically result in idealized portrayals of spiritualists communing with nature or bigoted descriptions of savages incapable of living in civilized society. Lost in these unfortunate images is the rich variety of customs, beliefs, and values that comprised—and still comprise—many of North America's native populations.

The *Indigenous Peoples of North America* series strives to present a complex, realistic picture of the many and varied Native American cultures. Each book in the series offers historical perspectives as well as a view of contemporary life of individual tribes and tribes that share a common region. The series examines traditional family life, spirituality, interaction with other native and non-native peoples, warfare, and the ways the environment shaped the lives and cultures of North America's indigenous populations. Each book ends with a discussion of life today for the Native Americans of a given region or tribe.

In any discussion of the Native American experience, there are bound to be similarities. All tribes share a past filled with unceasing white expansion and resistance that led to more than four hundred years of conflict. One U.S. administration after another pursued this goal and fought Indians who attempted to defend their homelands and ways of life. Although no war was ever formally declared, the U.S. policy of conquest precluded any chance of white and Native American peoples living together peacefully. Between 1780 and 1890, Americans killed hundreds of thousands of Indians and wiped out whole tribes.

The Indians lost the fight for their land and ways of life, though not for lack of bravery, skill, or a sense of purpose. They simply could not contend with the overwhelming numbers of whites arriving from Europe or the superior weapons they brought with them. Lack of unity also contributed to the defeat of the Native Americans. For most, tribal identity was more important than racial identity. This loyalty left the Indians at a distinct disadvantage. Whites had a strong racial identity and they fought alongside each other even when there was disagreement because they shared a racial destiny.

Although all Native Americans share this tragic history they have many distinct differences. For example, some tribes and individuals sought to cooperate almost immediately with the U.S. government while others steadfastly resisted the white presence. Life before the arrival of white settlers also varied. The nomads of the Plains developed altogether different lifestyles and customs from the fishermen of the Northwest coast.

Contemporary life is no different in this regard. Many Native Americans—forced onto reservations by the American government—struggle with poverty, poor health, and inferior schooling. But others have regained a sense of pride in themselves and their heritage, enabling them to search out new routes to self-sufficiency and prosperity.

The *Indigenous Peoples of North America* series attempts to capture the differences as well as similarities that make up the experiences of North America's native populations—both past and present. Fully documented primary and secondary source quotations enliven the text. Sidebars highlight events, personalities, and traditions. Bibliographies provide readers with ideas for further research. In all, each book in this dynamic series provides students with a wealth of information as well as launching points for further research.

Seeking a New Home

Like those to come after them the first Americans were immigrants. They came from places all over the vast Asian continent. They were a mixed people differing not only in culture, language, and lifestyle, but also in physical characteristics. Some were tall and thin, others stocky and thick boned. Some had narrow heads and hawklike noses, others were broad faced with wide, flat noses. Still, most shared certain characteristics reminiscent of their Asian heritage, such as dark or reddish brown skin, dark hair, little or no beard, and dark eyes. These travelers spread across North America, eventually establishing new civilizations that reflected a blend of their Asian heritage, the influence of other people they met along the way, and the dictates of the land.

Strong evidence suggests that the people who would come to be known as the Apache came late in this migration, arriving in the North American Southwest between

The people known as the Apache settled the Southwest hundreds of years ago.

A.D. 1300 and 1600. However, many Apache, even today, do not accept this theory. They believe simply that the Apache have always been a part of the deserts and mountains of the American Southwest. The study of the ancient history of any people is inexact, and much is left to interpretation. However, anthropologists believe the evidence supports the belief that the Apache came from Asia into Canada, across the plains, and finally into the American Southwest.

Anthropologists sometimes call the Apache Southern Athapaskans, because they speak a language in the Athapaskan family of languages. Their language identifies them as descendants of the last major linguistic group to migrate to this continent from Asia. Through artifacts, culture, and the Athapaskan language, scholars can connect the Apache people of the American Southwest with their ancient Asian heritage.

However the Apache came to be in the American Southwest, they eventually dominated a large area. Their homelands took in large parts of modern-day Arizona and New Mexico and extended north into Utah and Colorado and south into Texas and Mexico. Although they occupied a large territory, their numbers were never large; they did not build powerful political and cultural societies; they did not construct homes or temples that

The Apache came to be feared because of their skill and prowess as warriors.

would speak to future generations; they did not carve images in stone to greet the coming centuries. Yet they made an impression as powerful as any group to inhabit the New World. Around the world the name Apache evokes images of bravery and savagery, for theirs is the story of a determined people fighting to save their way of life.

Over a span of about three hundred years a few men armed with bows and arrows or inferior rifles faced well-equipped armies of Spanish, Mexican, and finally American troops. They were the last of the indigenous people of North America to put down their weapons and admit defeat. They continued to reign as wild Indians in the minds of the American people, even as many of them were carted across the country to face prison and the indignity of being exhibited as tourist attractions.

The remnants of this society now live quietly on and off reservations. Although a small minority in the United States today, the Apache are still struggling to retain their cultural heritage and to honor the ancient traditions of their proud ancestors.

Chapter 1

Adapting to a New Land

In the beginning Yusn, the Life-giver, created the Universe. Nobody knows just how he did it, but he did it and that is all.
   —Apache creation belief as told to James L. Haley, *Apaches: A History and Culture Portrait*

They called themselves "the People." In small family groups, they came out of Asia across the Bering Strait and into what is now Alaska. They brought their language, their culture, and their spiritual traditions. No one knows why they came, or why they were drawn ever farther southward. They may have been following the great herds of game, or escaping hostile neighbors. They were traditionally nomadic people; moving on came naturally to them. For hundreds of years, they inched southward away from the arctic winters, until at last they found their home in the sunwashed mountains, prairies, and deserts of what is now the vast American Southwest.

They would settle here, and for three hundred years would dominate the area.

They wanted a place to hunt, raise their families, cherish the land, and worship their god. They built, instead, a reputation as daring, vengeful, and ruthless warriors. They gained a new name that came to symbolize savagery to people around the world. They were the Apache.

The Land

When the Athapaskans arrived in the Southwest they found a land that was warmer than their northern homeland, but the climate was still harsh. In winter, icy winds and blowing snow whipped through the mountains and across the prairies. Summer brought intense heat and dry winds that drove clouds of dust and sand across the prairies. This was a land of craggy mountains jutting out of flat arid prairies and deserts cracked open by deep ravines and riverbeds. The land was laced by rivers, but their life-giving moisture clung close to their banks, creating narrow oases snaking across the desert. Some of the rivers dried up for months at a time, and at other times became raging torrents ripping out trees and sweeping along anything in their path.

Though mostly arid, the land was not barren. In the mountains, stands of evergreens such as pine, pinyon, and juniper were plentiful. The low country was carpeted with grasses, cacti, giant century plants, and other plants adapted to survive on little water. Willows and cottonwoods grew near the rivers and springs. Small animals such as rabbits, reptiles, birds, and insects abounded in the grasses and shrubs. Herds of bison grazed where the land joined the Great Plains of middle America. Elk, deer, and bighorn sheep roamed the prairies and mountains.

To some it might seem a harsh and inhospitable land, but it suited the nomadic lifestyle of the Athapaskans. They were accustomed to following the herds of game and the seasons of the wild food plants. The land did not invite agriculture, but some Athapaskan tribes, especially those on the eastern fringe of the territory, tried their hand at growing crops. For most, farming never became a mainstay of their existence. Instead, agriculture served only to supplement hunting and the gathering of wild vegetation. The farming groups had a

Although considered inhospitable by most people, the Southwest is an area that is full of grasses, cacti, and other useful desert plants.

base of operations where they grew their crops, but they were still nomads who spent most of the year on the move.

Neighbors

If the Athapaskans had been the first to discover this rugged land, they might have settled into an idyllic life of peace and relative plenty. Instead, they found the area already populated by many other groups of people, mostly small groups who lived nomadic lives very similar to the Athapaskan way. Others, such as the Pueblo people, had lived in the Southwest for thousands of years in stable communities of permanent adobe dwellings. They raised sheep and grew crops using innovative methods to make the land productive with a minimum amount of water. As explained in *People of the Desert*, these early residents represented a way of life that was foreign to the Apache:

> The travelers must have been astonished by the sights that greeted them. Across the sunbaked landscape of present-day Colorado, New Mexico, and Arizona, the nomads encountered large communities of Pueblo Indians living in sprawling adobe dwellings, some of which housed hundreds of people. Rather than depend solely on the vagaries of nature for food, these villagers had joined seed and soil, and broad fields of corn, cotton, beans, and squash surrounded their settlements, while the men tended the crops, their wives ground corn, wove mats and baskets, and molded clay

pots with striking red, white, and black markings.[1]

Other Native Americans were not the only ones to present strange new sights to the wandering Apache. By the time they arrived in the Southwest, Spanish explorers and settlers were already making their way north through Mexico, and Anglo-American settlers from the east would soon be trekking westward seeking to expand their holdings in the New World.

The land was vast, but its resources were sparsely spread over rugged terrain. Competition for game and water was bound to develop. And the Athapaskans soon proved themselves to be formidable adversaries. In fact, the most prevalent theory about the origin of the name Apache says it comes from the Zuni word *Apachu*, meaning "the Enemy."

The Apache Identity

The Apache, who came simply as "the People" and stayed to reign as "the Enemy," are not one group but many, loosely bound by ties of language, background, religious beliefs, and family connections. They form seven distinct tribes: the Western Apache, Chiricahua, Mescalero, Lipan, Jicarilla, Kiowa-Apache, and Navajo. In modern times the Navajo and Kiowa-Apache are not considered part of the Apache culture; because their lifestyles followed a different path, today they are recognized as distinct and separate groups.

The Apache groups or tribes are further broken down into bands. For example,

The Telltale Tongue

Anthropologists use several types of clues to trace the movements of early peoples. One of these telltale clues is language. By the time the Athapaskans arrived, hundreds of languages were spoken on the American continent. Linguists can divide these many languages into related groups, or families. Languages are living things. They grow and change to fit the needs of the people who use them, but they always retain characteristics of their origin. For example, English-speaking people cannot understand French, but the two languages have enough in common to identify them as being part of the Indo-European family of languages.

As the Athapaskans moved southward they left a trail of not only scattered arti-facts of their existence, but bands of Athapaskan-speaking people who chose to settle and travel no more. Linguists can follow this thread of language. It has evolved and changed from group to group, but can still be identified as Athapascan. One end of the thread reaches deep into the ancient civilizations of Asia, the other wends its way out of the far northern woodlands into the American Great Plains and southward to the Apache tribes of the Southwest.

When languages have evolved only slightly, the new versions are called dialects. The different Apache tribes speak different dialects. Some of their words and grammar constructions are different, but they can still understand each other.

Geronimo, famed warrior and medicine man of the Chiricahua, led a band called the Nde-nda-i. A band usually consists of several clans that in turn comprise several extended families. The family is the central unit of Apache life. Bands, clans, and extended families usually have their own names, a fact that has lent confusion to studies of the boundaries of Apache territory and culture. To further complicate matters, in early writings the word *Apache* was sometimes used for Indian groups not remotely related to the Athapaskan Apache.

The many different groups and group names contributed to confusion about just how many Apache there actually were. Early writers tended to greatly overestimate their numbers. What we know about Apache history was recorded not by Apache historians but by their enemies. It made better reading if a settler lost his horses to five hundred wild Apaches rather than to two dozen stealthy night raiders. James Haley compares these inflated estimates:

Their ferocity and reputation cast a shadow far beyond their size, and the early white transients and settlers who lived in that shadow frequently over guessed their strength by large if understandable exaggerations. The usually unflappable John Cremony, who lived among the Chiricahuas in the mid–nineteenth century, believed there was an all-told sum of 25,000 Apaches. The easily flapped George Catlin thought there were 30,000. In point of fact, vast Apacheria (the Apache land) probably never contained more than 10,000 of the Tinne-'ah (the people), and the true figure lies more likely between 6,000 and 8,000.[2]

The Apache themselves probably had no idea of their total number and had little interaction with other Apache tribes. However, the various Apache groups shared many traits carried down through their common heritage.

Different Life-Ways, All Reflecting the Land

All Apache lived similar nomadic lifestyles and relied heavily on hunting and gathering to make their living. This was both the traditional Athapaskan way of life and the lifestyle best supported by the land. Deeply rooted Athapakan religious beliefs and rituals remained similar for all Apache groups.

A lack of strong tribal organization was typical of all of the Apache. Groups came together on occasion in tribal meetings, or for religious ceremonies, but there was no central government or structured system of leadership. Each family made its own decisions and could choose to join with the others or not. All Apache families were matrilocal, which simply means that newly married couples lived near the wife's family.

In spite of many similarities, Apache lifestyles varied. This vast new land had many faces and each group adapted to its circumstances. There were three general, and often overlapping, lifestyles among the Apache. The homes they constructed tell a lot about how they lived.

For example, in their journey south, the Apache learned much from the plains people. They became skilled buffalo hunters, and some chose to settle permanently within the range of the buffalo herds. The Lipan, in particular, remained plains people. Their economy was based on the buffalo, and their homes mimicked the tipis of their neighbors. The Mescalero and Jicarilla were also influenced by the plains lifestyle and preferred tipis, but theirs were usually not as large or as well constructed as those of the true plains people.

Tipis

Tipis were ingeniously designed buffalo-skin tents, the exteriors often decorated with symbolic artwork. The women of the tribe constructed the tipis of wooden poles and buffalo skins. They lashed several poles about 20 feet long together near the top. They spread the poles out tripod fashion and more poles were added to complete the framework. They completed the job by stretching a cover, made of ten or more buffalo hides sewn together, over this framework. An opening in the top let the smoke out and another at the base served as a door.

Artist and historian Thomas E. Mails has written and illustrated several books on American Indians, including the Apache. In praise of the ingenuity of the tipi he writes that

the buffalo hide tipi and all of its contents easily deserve a place among the world's leading examples of classic mobile design. Averaging fourteen feet in diameter and large enough to house an average family of five to eight persons, it could be set up by a woman in less than fifteen minutes and taken down in three. The homes and furnishings of an entire camp could be packed upon horse or dog-drawn travois [sled] and on the move in twenty minutes. The tipi, assisted by only a brush fence, carried its occupants through the worst winters using minimum fuel, and with rolled-up sides became a

The Apache constructed their homes according to their lifestyle. The hogan (pictured) was designed as a more permanent dwelling.

vented summer umbrella. During the day its translucent walls admitted a pleasant light, and at night each dwelling transformed itself into a giant candle to illuminate the camp. It required no painting, save decoration, and was repaired simply by patching.[3]

Despite the advantages of the tipi, Apache who left the plains for areas where buffalo hides were not plentiful found other building styles, such as the hogan and the wickiup, better adapted to their lifestyle and their environment.

Hogans

As the life-way of the Navajo diverged from the Apache and they became settled ranchers and farmers, they preferred a dwelling called a hogan, a more permanent home constructed of logs or stone and covered with earth. Hogans were usually windowless, but had a vent in the roof to let out the smoke from their heating and cooking fires. The design of the hogan was influenced by the Pueblo people living in the area. However, hogans were always stand-alone units, rather than the large apartment-type complexes built by the Pueblo.

Most Apache, however, roamed the deserts and mountains far from the buffalo herds. They still relied heavily on hunting, with deer replacing the buffalo as their favorite game animal. In general, game here was smaller and less plentiful than on the plains; thus, large hides were hard to come by, and in addition the tipis were cumber-

some to move around in the more rugged terrain of the Southwest. The tribes of the deserts and mountains used neither tipis nor hogans. Instead, they preferred a type of dwelling they could simply abandon when it was time to move.

The Wickiup

The wickiup, the most typical Apache home, was a shelter adapted to the environment and the lifestyle of nomadic desert and mountain people. Though the basic design was consistent, completed dwellings varied in appearance and materials depending on what was available in the area. As with tipis, it was the woman's job to construct and furnish the dwelling.

Morris Edward Opler, whose extensive early research on the Chiracahua Apache has proved invaluable, recorded numerous interviews in the 1920s and 1930s with Apache who still had clear memories of the old way of life. One of Opler's sources reports that

the woman not only makes the furnishings of the home but is responsible for the construction, maintenance, and repair of the dwelling itself and for the arrangement of everything in it. She provides the grass and brush beds and replaces them when they become too old and dry. With a stiff grass broom or with a leafy branch, she sweeps out the interior if that is necessary. However, formerly "they had no permanent homes, so they didn't bother with cleaning."[4]

The Comforts of Home

Furniture in the Apache household was spartan. Some of it, like the wickiup itself, would be abandoned with each move. Typical amenities included wooden frames built on poles that elevated a sleeper's bed two feet or so off the dirt floor. This framework was padded with brush and dry grass and covered with blankets.

Kitchen utensils consisted of a clay pot or two, a water jug, scraping and cutting implements, and a mano, or grinding stone, used with a stone slab, or metate, to grind corn or seeds. Contact with Europeans brought the addition of metal implements such as skillets and knives.

Baskets of various types were essential for food gathering and sometimes intricately beaded bags served ceremonial purposes.

The wickiup was a dome-shaped structure with a framework of poles or saplings. The women thatched over the frame with whatever plant material was available—yucca leaves or scrub in the desert, grass in the prairies, or brush in the mountains. The completed shelter was about seven feet high at the center peak and anywhere from eight to fifteen feet in diameter. There was a low hide-covered opening for a door, usually oriented to face east be-

cause this was considered the sacred direction. In the winter, skins (and in later years, canvas) were stretched over the outside of the wickiup to provide more protection from the elements. When it was time to move on, the Apaches abandoned the wickiup, and built another one in the next place, using whatever materials were locally available.

Whether they lived in a tipi, a wickiup, or a hogan, most Apache also built a structure the Spanish called a ramada. The ramada was an open-air shelter supported by four large posts connected by crossbeams with a thatched top. Much of the day was spent working or relaxing in the shade of the ramada. Like the wickiup, the ramada was left behind when it was time to move on.

A Moving-Day Innovation: The Dog Travois

In the very early days, moving was difficult no matter which type of housing was preferred. The people walked and carried their personal possessions and household goods. Later, probably through early contact with Europeans, they were introduced to dogs and found a way to lighten their load on moving day.

They built small A-shaped frames that the French called travois, harnessed the dogs to the sleds, and piled household goods on them. In spite of their usefulness as pack animals and later as stock herders, dogs were never viewed affectionately by the Apache. Opler quotes an Apache's remark about dogs: "The dog was classed with the coyote, wolf, and fox. We felt that all of them could cause you trouble. We wouldn't touch the skin of a dead dog. When you have a disease from a dog, the saliva comes down as it does with a mad dog. You get a little crazy and go, 'Aaaa!'"[5]

With dogs as pack animals, moving became easier. Still, people could count as permanent possessions only as much as they and their dogs could move. Soon, however, the Spaniards introduced an animal that would transform Apache society.

Mystery Dogs

Before the coming of the Spanish, horses were unknown—the only domestic ani-mals kept by the Apache or other Indians were dogs. So when the Spaniards arrived astride their horses, the Apache called the animals mystery dogs or sometimes just big dogs. The strange new animals would have a profound impact on many of the indigenous peoples of the Americas. The Apache were probably the first Native Americans to acquire horses: They stole them from the Spanish, and ate them.

As a source of food, horses were a welcome innovation. Fresh wild game was a periodic treat. The hunters had to track the game, kill it, butcher it on the spot, and pack the meat back to camp. Once back in camp they had to eat the game soon, or

The wickiup was constructed from whatever materials were available in the area and was abandoned when the family moved on to other locations.

dry and preserve it. Horses, however, could simply be stolen from the Spanish, driven back to camp, and kept in pens until they were needed.

The Apache soon discovered the added advantages of horses: Until it was time to butcher them for food, the animals could be ridden or used as beasts of burden. Horses proved to be much more efficient pack animals than dogs. Warriors could cover more ground on horseback than on foot, and could make a quick getaway after a raid. The value of the horse was enhanced by the fact that it ate grass rather than valuable meat.

Indians or Native Americans

When Christopher Columbus landed in the New World, he mistakenly thought he was in the East Indies, so he called the people he found living there Indians. The name stuck and came to include the many diverse cultures occupying North and South America.

According to the Bureau of Indian Affairs (BIA) website, the term "Native American" came into usage in the 1960s to denote the groups served by the BIA. It included American Indians and the Alaska Natives (Indians, Eskimos, and Aleut). Later the term included Native Hawaiians and Pacific Islanders; as broadened, the name came into disfavor among some North American Indian groups.

Today some prefer to be called Native Americans, others First People, still others Amerindians or American Indians. All of these terms have as their point of reference the rich variety of cultures existing in the Americas before the arrival of the first Europeans. To most the name by which they are known is not a major issue as long as it is used with respect for their rich cultural diversity and contributions to the history of the Americas.

Upon arriving in the New World, Christopher Columbus mistakenly called the people he encountered Indians.

Through trade and warfare, the Apache helped spread horses throughout the Southwest and into the plains. The buffalo hunters of the plains were quick to recognize the significant advantage in mobility that the horse offered. They valued their horses highly, cared for them, and rarely ate horse meat. For most Apache, however, the horse remained a choice source of food as well as transportation. This different attitude may explain why they never developed the level of equestrian skill of the Plains Indians.

With the coming of the horse, not only meat but other foods became more readily available. On horseback the women gatherers could reach stands of wild plant foods more quickly, and transport larger loads back to camp. Food was plentiful and life was good. The excess meat and hides encouraged trade with neighboring peoples. But more important was the fact that this economic abundance gave young braves and warriors time to turn their attention to the activities that the Apache would become best known for—raiding and warfare.

While the men benefited with extra time for other pursuits, their wives were burdened with the additional chores of processing the abundant food supplies. In fact, many Apache men took a second or even a third

The Apache quickly learned to use the horse for a wide variety of purposes.

wife because one woman could not handle the job of processing all of the meat and by-products. Additional wives were usually sisters of the first wife, and the help was welcomed by the first wife. More than one wife in a family was a sign of wealth and prestige. More wives also meant more children, and "children were greatly prized and treasured, both for their own sakes and as economic assets."[6]

Chapter 2

Growing Up Apache

Life in an Apache camp was a subtle blend of age-old traditions, religious beliefs, and adaptations to the needs of the day. It was important for the young Apache to begin early to learn the Apache life-way. The Apache had no schools and no written language. Apache children were taught through legends, songs, religious ceremonies, and example. It was important that they be taught well, because the survival of the family and the clan depended on each individual understanding his role in society. Though strict in teaching life skills, the Apache loved their children and treated them with gentleness and often indulgence.

Preparing for a New Life

Even before a baby was born, the Apache expressed their love of children by showing extra respect and consideration for the expectant mother. When a woman became pregnant she took steps to assure the safe delivery of a healthy child. She did not ride a horse, overexert herself, or lift heavy loads. She followed dietary advice and especially avoided fatty meats. She abstained from sex throughout her pregnancy and until she weaned the child. She was, however, still expected to perform routine household chores. Opler quotes one of his Apache sources:

> The consideration with which she is treated reflects the great love of children that characterizes the society. "A woman about to become a mother is treated extra nice, just like a child." Yet the performance of ordinary household tasks is considered beneficial to her throughout this period, and laziness and self-pity are ridiculed. "They say that when you sit on the child after the fifth month it will be harder for you. The child gets in the right position for coming out if you move around. The more you are a coward about it, the worse it will be for you."[7]

The birth of the new baby was an important event attended by the mother's female relatives and her husband's female relatives if they happened to live nearby.

Among these women there was usually one who was skilled as a midwife and who had earned the right to perform birth ceremonies. Haley describes her duties:

Almost immediately after the birth, the midwife-diyin (medicine woman) began the birth ceremony, rinsing the infant in lukewarm water. If it had been crying loudly the water might be mixed with an extract of Parosela formosa (a medicinal plant) to quiet it. Commonly a newborn was rubbed with a mixture of red ocher [clay] and grease, then wrapped in a soft blanket. The specific prayers and incantations depended on the personal method and power of the midwife, but usually the ceremony included the sprinkling of ha-dintin pollen or ashes to the four directions, beginning with the east, and then on the child.[8]

The new baby was given a name, often one suggested by the midwife. This "baby name" would be changed later in life to one more suited to the developing individual. An Apache father speaks about the naming process:

When my daughter was born, the midwife gave her a name, but it did not catch on. Then my wife called her "My Daughter." All the others around our camp now do so too. Later, before she is ten or eleven years old, we will give her another name. This is a Chiricahua custom. The baby name is outgrown. One child, for example is called "Ugly Baby" but she will not be called this later on. Later the child will be named according to circumstances; something about the child will suggest a name.[9]

Baby Days

Soon after birth, usually on the fourth day, the new baby was strapped into a cradleboard where it would spend most of its time for the next few months. Care and

For the first few months of its life, an Apache baby spent the majority of its time strapped onto a cradleboard.

ceremony went into building the cradle-board. First, a strong wood such as oak or walnut was chosen to construct the frame-work. The crosspieces on the back were a more pliable material. According to one of Opler's sources, "For the back part of the cradleboard, the cross-pieces are of sotol if the cradle is for a boy, and of narrow-leafed yucca if it is for a girl. These plants are brother and sister, we say."[10]

Next, the builders chose a lightweight wood to make a canopy to shield the child's face, and stretched buckskin over the framework and canopy. The baby was placed on bedding of wild mustard or sedge. The appropriate area was stuffed with soft mosses to absorb the baby's waste. To protect the child from skin rashes, a type of baby powder was made from the bark of the heart-leafed willow. Finally, the new cradleboard was decorated with designs, amulets, and small baubles to both protect and amuse the child.

Strapping the baby in for the first time was an important ceremonial and social occasion. The parents hired a shaman, or di-yin, to perform the ceremony, which could be very elaborate or fairly simple, depending on the wealth of the family. The exact nature of the ceremony varied, but usually involved sprinkling pollen and pointing the baby to the four directions.

Getting Around

When a child became too large and too ac-tive for the cradleboard, he or she began to crawl around and explore the camp, always, of course, under the watchful eye of adults.

Every stage of development was celebrated with rituals and ceremonies. One ceremony celebrated the first steps, another the first haircut. In the spring after the little girl or boy left the cradleboard, the di-yin cut the child's hair short, leaving a few patches of long strands. Haley writes: "After such a ceremony it was thought excessively funny for the adults to tease the children that they looked like quail."[11] This ceremonial hair-cutting was repeated for four springs in a row. After the fourth spring the hair was al-lowed to grow; cutting it after this time could bring bad luck.

The Apache child learned about the beliefs and traditions of his people through partici-pating in and observing these and other im-portant ceremonies. He also began to learn lessons of survival. For example, the young child had to learn how to be absolutely quiet and still when necessary. The Apache were often at war and in hiding. A crying baby could bring disaster to the camp:

Babies were taught very early the value of silence. If an infant sought at-tention by crying, it was taken from the rancheria (camp), strung from a bush, and ignored until it became quiet. Ap-proval was restored after that. Crying babies could give away the location of a rancheria to a raiding enemy, or foul an attempt to escape. In terrible emer-gencies it was not unknown, when the survival of the group depended on it, to kill crying babies, or even ones with a reputation for sudden tantrums, when hiding from an enemy.[12]

Coiffures: Style and Social Significance

Their glossy dark hair was not only a source of pride to Apache women but a potential message of availability to suitors. James Haley describes hair care and styles in his book *Apaches: A History and Culture Portrait.*

"Apache women gave considerable attention to their hair, shampooing it with lather from an aloe called soapweed, brushing it with tips of grass bristles, and spreading it on outstretched arms to dry. For virgins or unmarried women among the Western Apaches, the hair was vertically bundled at the nape of the neck and wrapped in the nah-leen, or hair bow. This was a piece of leather shaped like a bow or hourglass, worn vertically with the upper and lower loops decoratively studded with beads or brass knobs. The strands that fastened the nah-leen to the hair were usually of brightly colored cloth and hung well down the back. When a woman married, she destroyed the hair bow and let her hair cascade down her back and shoulders, shaped off squarely at the bottom. Failure to destroy the hair bow at marriage was a serious insult to her husband, signifying as it did that she might take lovers.

Among the Chiricahuas the nah-leen was fashion, without significance to a woman's status or sexual availability. A particularly rich or important Chiricahua woman might have her hair groomed by her female slave-captives, and the hair bow was generally worn until the woman was sufficiently advanced in years to give little further thought to her hair."

Thomas Mails cites reports of infanticide in cases of babies who either were feeble or cried excessively. However, not all of the Apache child's training had life-or-death implications, and many childhood lessons have a universal ring. One Apache remembers his training in etiquette:

As far back as I can remember my father and mother directed me how to act. They used to tell me, "Do not use a bad word which you wouldn't like to be used to you. . . . In playing with children remember this: do not take anything from another child. Don't take arrows away from another boy just because you are bigger than he is. Don't take his marbles away. Don't steal from your own friends. Don't be unkind to your playmates. . . .

"When you go to the creek and swim, don't duck anyone's children. . . .

"Don't laugh at feeble old men and women. That's the worst thing you can do. Don't criticize them and make fun of them. Don't laugh at anybody or make fun of anybody. . . .

"When you start to eat, act like a grown person. Just wait until things are served to you. Do not take bread or a drink or a piece of meat before the rest start to eat. Don't ask before the meal for things that are still cooking, as many children do. . . . Try to be just as polite as you can; sit still while you eat. . . .

"Don't run into another person's camp as though it was your own. . . . When you go to another camp, don't stand at the door. Go right in and sit down like a grown person. Don't get into their drinking water. Don't go out and catch or hobble horses and ride them as if they belonged to you the way some boys do. Do not throw stones at anybody's animals. When a visitor comes, do not go in front of him or step over him. Do not cut up while the visitor is here. If you want to play, get up quietly, go behind the visitor, and out the door.[13]

When children disobeyed, parents avoided corporal punishment if possible. Instead they tried to control a child's behavior by ridicule or by scaring the little boy or girl with warn-

Apache children quickly learned all about life from their parents and other adults.

ings drawn from traditional ceremonial figures or mythical beings. For example, the Clown, who accompanied the dancers in certain rituals, was said to punish bad children, and was used as a threat to misbehaving children. The Coyote stories were also used to influence behavior of both children and adults. Coyote was said to have done all of the bad things that could be done, and the many stories about his exploits were used to show the folly of bad behavior. Opler quotes an Apache source: "Coyote stories are used as a lesson. And they still blame Coyote today for the foolish things humans do."[14]

Learning Life Roles

For the first few years Apache boys and girls played together, and practiced their future life roles. Both men and women were well respected in the Apache culture, but their responsibilities in the family and the group were distinct and separate, and these differences were reflected in childhood make-believe. Playing house was popular among Apache children. They built scaled-down wickiups and furnished them with miniature versions of the things they saw in their own homes. The boys, pretending to be men, would go out to hunt with toy bows and arrows made from reeds, while the girls prepared make-believe food and cared for homemade dolls. When

Apache girls were expected to help around camp and learn their roles as future wives and mothers.

boys were six or seven years old they pulled away from this domestic play with the girls and joined older boys for pretend hunts and war parties.

As girls grew, they played less and helped their mothers more around the camp. By the time they reached puberty they were well skilled in the business of running a household. Following the elaborate girl's puberty ceremony they were considered women ready to assume an

Preparing Versatile Animal Skins

The preservation of animal hides was a woman's responsibility and required great skill. The exact method of preserving depended on the eventual use of the skin. For example, the hair was left on skins destined to be blankets, and special attention was given to the softness and appearance of a skin that would become buckskin clothing. The Apache made some skins into thick, stiff rawhide, a very useful material when toughness and durability were important.

Whatever the final use, the first step was always to scrape away the flesh adhering to the inner surface. A sharpened bone or stone was used before knives became available. Then the skin had to be soaked for several days to loosen the fur if it was to be removed. Next it was hung over a log propped diagonally against a tree trunk, and the hair was carefully scraped off with a sharpened

horse rib. The skin was then stretched and pegged to dry in the sun for another few days.

To make soft pliable buckskin out of deer hides, the women made a tanning paste from a mixture of fat and deer brains that they worked to the desired consistency with their hands. Next they worked the paste into the rawhide until the skin began to soften. When it was pliable enough, it was again hung in the sun for a short while. Finally it was further softened by pulling and stretching. James Haley quotes an Apache source who describes the process: "She works it all over and on both sides as it dries. If she starts early in the morning, she gets through about noon with this stretching. Once in a while she stops and lets it dry some more. By the time she is finished, it has turned into buckskin."

adult position as wife and mother. They could now marry and build their own wickiup or tipi within the camp of their mother, where they would continue to share help and advice with their mother and sisters.

Women Were Homemakers

As an adult the woman played a very important role in camp life. She was responsible for building the dwelling; that

dwelling and all of the household goods and utensils in it belonged to her. Food gathering and preparation was her job. She both gathered and processed nuts, berries, and plants for food, medicine, and basket making. She ground acorns and berries into flour or a paste that could be stored for future use. The woman also prepared the meat and animal by-products brought home by her hunter husband. The meat was cooked and eaten immediately or dried for later use. The dried meat was made into jerky or pulverized and mixed with nuts and berries to make a nutritious mixture called pemmican.

The wife also processed the skins, bladders, and bones of the game for a variety of uses. She made buckskin or rawhide from the animal hides, and fashioned skins into clothing, blankets, and containers. The bones were cleaned and made into tools such as knives, scrapers, and awls for sewing.

Containers of various types were always in demand around the camp. The women made containers from animal skins and bladders, dried gourds, clay, and any material suitable for basket making. Apache women did not develop great skill in pottery making; their vessels were usually simple and undecorated. In contrast, they were well known for their basket-weaving skills:

Crafted from plant parts—usually yucca, sumac, and mulberry—and often embellished with strands dyed red, blue, and yellow, Apache baskets are finely woven, with a simple utilitarian elegance. Traditionally, three types were produced—round, shallow trays used for parching seeds and sifting grain; tall, flat-bottomed burden baskets for transporting and storing goods; and amphora-like vessels for holding water and tiswin, a mild beer the Apache brew from freshly sprouted corn. Apache women prided themselves on these watertight containers, which they sealed by smearing melted pitch from the pinon tree over the interior of a woven basket.[15]

While the women taught homemaking skills to their daughters and worked to keep the family fed and clothed and the rancheria, or camp, running smoothly, their older sons were busy preparing to be hunters and warriors.

A Man's Job

When a boy was seven or eight years old he began learning the skills of his father, for it would one day be his job to protect and provide meat for his family and to wage war on their enemies. The youngsters watched the men of the clan, and learned the secrets of making weapons. They learned that well-crafted weapons were not only a source of pride, but often the key to survival. They made miniature bows and other weapons for actual use or as toys, and developed skill at hunting birds and other small game. Cultural historian Opler describes this early process:

The boy whips pellets of mud, lightly stuck at the end of a willow branch, at birds and achieves considerable accuracy with this weapon. He soon learns to make good use of the sling, a diamond-shaped piece of hide to which one looped and one unlooped side thong are attached. The hide is folded over upon itself, encasing a stone which is projected when the sling is swung forward. A piece of elderberry, ash, reed, or walnut from which the pith has been removed, or through which a hole has been worked, is made into a popgun by tamping one end and forcing another piece through until the tamp flies out with a loud report.[16]

In addition to learning the skills of weaponry and hunting, young boys "learned courage and daring through the rough games they played with other boys, through stirring

A number of activities prepared Apache boys to become skilled hunters and warriors.

communal rituals of song and dance that celebrated feats of war, and through lessons instilled in them by their mothers, sisters, and sweethearts, who cherished bravery in a man above all else."[17]

Mothers often encouraged their sons to run up steep mountains, swim in icy streams, and endure other hardships so that they would grow to be brave, strong men. This training and conditioning had the desired effect because most boys were eager to join the men on their first hunt and eventually become a member of a war party.

The boys became tough and strong. As men they ruled the deserts and mountains. They were masters of hunting, raiding, and warfare, feared across the Southwest. But back in the camp their dominance was not as well established:

When an Apache couple married, the new husband typically joined his wife's family—and, from that point on, exhibited a healthy deference to his new in-laws. Depending on the group, custom dictated that an Apache man never speak directly to his in-laws, or at the extreme, never allow himself to be in the presence of his wife's mother.[18]

Spring Feast, Winter Sustenance

Spring was a time of rejoicing and industry among Apache women. Supplies of food dried the previous summer were almost depleted when new life began coming to the earth. One of the first food plants to appear was the yucca, a plant in the agave family, also called Spanish bayonet for its sharp swordlike leaves. The first shoots were gathered while they were still green and tender, roasted until they were soft, peeled, and eaten immediately. Older, thicker stalks were pounded and steamed by piling them on hot stones with a layer of fresh grass on top to hold in the moisture. Stalks cooked this way could be sun-dried and kept for future use. A little later in the spring the clusters of white flowers were gathered and boiled with meat to make a stew.

After the yucca, the mescal sprouted. Mescal, another agave also known as century plant, was so important in the diet of many Apache that, if none grew nearby, the women would travel long distances and set up temporary camps to harvest it. The stalks were roasted like yucca, but the lower portion or crown was even more important as a food source. The women dug a large pit and lined it with rocks for baking the crowns. The pit was filled with wood and more stones were put on top. Prayers were offered and the fire lit ceremoniously on all four sides starting with the east. When the wood burned down, the woman put the mescal in and topped it with wet grass and dirt to form a steamer oven. Mescal is a very large plant and the cooking took from two to four days.

Some of the mescal was eaten freshly roasted and some was dried. The soft centers of the leaves were pounded into thin sheets, dried, and glazed with mescal juice that served as a preservative. With a good supply of dried mescal, the family was assured of food for the winter months.

Love and Marriage

Marriage among the Apache was usually an economic arrangement. However, the young people did have some say in their choice of mate. Prior to marriage arrangements, usually the girl initiated a flirtation. She might choose a young man she liked as her partner at a social dance. Sometimes an aunt or other female relative would go to a dance with her and point out young men of good character and family.

If the young brave shared the girl's feelings, he would let his father or an uncle know that he was attracted to the girl. If the older man considered this a suitable match, he would approach the girl's father. Negotiations took place between the two families and if they reached an agreement, the young man presented the girl's family with gifts—often several horses with saddles and bridles.

Once the gifts were offered and accepted, the girl and her female relatives built a dwelling for the young couple in the camp of her mother. The marriage was not celebrated with any kind of formal wedding ceremony, but sometimes a feast was held when the new groom moved into his in-laws' camp. After they were married, if the young couple were quite comfortable with each other, they might spend one to three weeks at a secluded camp the bridegroom had set up before returning to set up a household in the girl's family camp. Often, though, the new husband and wife were too shy and embarrassed to be alone together. Haley reports that some were

so terrified at the prospect of sleeping together that they prevailed upon sympathetic cross-cousins to stay with them at first. Night would find them four in the bed, the bride and groom on the outside, petrified and motionless; the groom's male cross-cousin slept next to him, the bride's

Fun and Games

The Apache were avid game players. They enjoyed a variety of games and usually bet on the outcome. Both men and women played card games using decks of cards made of thin rectangles of rawhide. A favorite game among the women was called stave. The object of this game was to move one's counter along a circle of stones. The number of spaces moved in each turn was decided by the throw of marked staves. The women often played this game while men were on the field engaged in their favorite game, and by far the most important game of the Apache, hoop and pole.

Hoop and pole was strictly a man's game. Not only were women forbidden to play, but they were not allowed to come near the grounds where it was being played. Haley describes the game in *Apaches: A History and Cultural Portrait:*

"In this game a small hoop somewhat more than a foot in diameter was rolled down a sort of alley, and just as it was about to fall, each of the two contestants slid his long, tapering pole after it in such a fashion as to cause the hoop to fall on the butt end of the piece [pole]. Both the hoop and the poles were notched with point markers, and a player accrued points based upon how many pole notches were within the hoop and how many knots on the hoop's crosspiece (a thong marked with knots or beads tied across the diameter of the hoop) were over the pole."

female cross-cousin between him and the bride. Tact and good judgement of the moment dictated when the cross-cousins would leave the newlyweds alone to face each other.[19]

When the young couple returned to the bride's family camp, the young man began learning the art of politely avoiding his mother-in-law, an important custom. Sometimes the mother-in-law was thoughtful enough to wear a bell or noisy bangles around her neck as a sort of early warning system for the young man.

The young man went to great pains to show proper respect and avoidance behavior toward his wife's relatives. Otherwise, he might be suspected of being a witch. This was a serious accusation in Apache culture, which centered around a strong belief in spirits, witches, and ghosts and the control these spirit beings had over every aspect of life.

Chapter 3

The Power Was Everywhere

The guiding force of Apache life was a deeply felt reverence for the supernatural powers of the universe. No one knows the exact origin of Apache religious belief. But we know that they lived in tune with the natural world. Their survival depended on understanding and respecting their environment, so it was natural to revere the great forces of nature.

The foundations of Apache belief probably came from stories, ceremonies, and symbols passed down from generation to generation by their Athapaskan ancestors. These basic beliefs were likely influenced by the plains people they met on their journey south and the Pueblo people they found already living in the Southwest. With no written language, they depended on memory and interpretation to preserve and pass on their religion. Not surprisingly, the details of Apache religious belief varied from group to group and even from shaman to shaman. However, basic beliefs and means of expression are universal among the Apache, and strong threads of similarity run through all Native American theology. As Cherokee Gregg Howard writes, "Almost every Indian culture believed that every mountain had a soul, every tree, every rock, every living creature and the Great Spirit flowed through all, keeping nature and mankind in perfect balance."[20] The Apache, like their fellow Native Americans, believed that spiritual power was everywhere.

The Powers of the Universe

The Apache believed in one god, whose name was Yusn (or Ussen), meaning Creator of Life. Supernatural power, however, was inherent in all things—in humans, wild animals, birds and insects, in plants and rocks and every grain of sand. Power resided in thunder, lightning, wind, and rain. The power was not, however, distributed evenly. Some things had greater power than others. Some had good power and were sacred sources of healing and prayer. Others had evil power and could bring sickness and misfortune to any who dared defy them. For example, owls were believed to be the earthly presence of the Evil Dead and were greatly feared. The powers of the bear, coyote, and snake were also suspect and fearsome.

Animal spirits exercised wide-ranging power, but the principal supernaturals, or culture heros, were White-Painted Woman, Killer of Enemies, and Child of the Water. White-Painted Woman might be called the mother of Apache culture. Haley writes that, "with Yusn in the beginning was White-painted Woman. She had no mother or father. She was created by the power of Yusn. He sent her down to the world to live. Her home was a cave."[21] The origin and identity of Killer of Enemies is not clear. He is variously described as White-Painted Woman's brother, her son, or occasionally even her husband. Child of the Water is clearly her

Modern American Indian Spirituality

In his book *Spirits of the Earth: A Guide to Native American Nature Symbols, Stories, and Ceremonies,* modern-day Native American spiritualist Bobby Lake–Thom relates his people's ancient beliefs about spirituality and natural healing not just to the individual but to the health of the earth.

"I believe we are all children of Nature. As a traditional Native healer, and like my mentors, I am not only concerned about individual healing cases and situations, but also about collective healing needs; healing of the individual in relation to the community, and healing of communities in relation to our environment. I am concerned about people gaining spiritual knowledge so that they can develop spiritually and heal their relationship with Earth and Nature. Otherwise we will continue to have a sick society. The Earth should not be treated as an enemy.

We cannot simply assume that we have sole dominion over our planet. The Earth is a living and breathing organism that we depend upon for survival. When we get out of balance with Nature and the Earth we become sick, and a lot of people are sick today because they have allowed their society and communities to harm, hurt, molest, torment, desecrate, and exploit Nature without just cause, to treat Nature without proper reciprocity. Life proceeds in a circle; what goes around comes around! So much has already been lost because of civilization, technological progress, industrial development, and pollution. With this desecration has come a loss of knowledge, values, and spirtuality. In the meantime, Nature cries out to us all for help. It is constantly communicating to all of us, but most people in modern society are not even aware of it, or they haven't learned how to interpret the communication."

son and was fathered by water or lightning. These three supernaturals and the story of the slaying of the monsters form the core of Apache mythology. Haley relates an Apache source's version of the myth of Child of the Water and the monsters:

Some say there were no other people in those days, but I don't know about it. They say that's what the monsters lived on, so there must have been some. There weren't many, though, and they had a real hard time.

There were four monsters. They killed people and ate them. They were Owl-man Giant, Buffalo Monster, the Eagle Monster family, and Antelope Monster.

As the story goes, Child of the Water proved himself to be the offspring of lightning by his fearlessness:

White-painted Woman took him outside. She told Lightning, "Your son knows you."

Lightning said, "How do I know this is my son?"

She answered, "Test him."

Lightning had him stand over to the east, and black lightning struck him. He stood to the south and blue lightning struck him. Yellow lightning struck him on the west, and white lightning on the north. Child of the Water was not hurt or frightened at all.[22]

After proving himself through his fearlessness, Child of the Water used powers given him by his father to find and slay the four monsters. The particulars vary from tribe to tribe, but this basic legend forms the core of Apache mythology.

All humans, as did all other things, had some degree of power, but certain chosen individuals had keenly developed powers

Lozen's Power

Lozen, sister of Chief Victorio, was a shaman as well as a respected female warrior. She called on supernatural powers to enable her to heal wounds and to locate the enemy. James Kawaykla, quoted in *Once They Moved Like the Wind* by David Roberts, remembered the prayer used by Lozen to summon her powers.

In this world Ussen has Power;
This Power He has granted me
For the good of my people.
This I see as one from a height
Sees in every direction;
This I feel as though I
Held in my palms
something that tingles.
This Power is mine to use,
But only for the good of my people.

As she sang she would slowly move in a circle until a tingling sensation in her palms signaled the enemy's location.

Because it was believed that they possessed extraordinary power, shamans (pictured), or medicine men, were highly honored and respected among the Apache.

and engaged in direct interaction with the supernatural. As one Apache put it, "What you can see is only a little of the whole thing. The power is in the spirit part. Some people can learn to reach the spirit part of something, and they become its shaman."[23]

Power Works Through Humans

People who possessed extraordinary power were known as di-yins, or in English, shamans or medicine men and women. They were usually specialists with powers granted to them only in certain areas. Along with the power, they were granted the privilege of performing the ceremonies and rituals associated with their particular spirit.

Other Apache respected these individuals because they were chosen by the power to represent it among humans. "No matter how eager a man is to acquire a ceremony, the first gesture is always attributed to the power, for power requires man for its complete expression and constantly seeks human beings through whom 'to work.'"[24]

Sometimes the shaman got his power directly from a spirit through a dream, vision, or extraordinary occurrence. Others gained their power through being tutored by another shaman, as Haley explains:

The ceremonies shamans performed often involved precise wording and actions in order to be effective.

Ceremonial power, like physical prowess, waned with the passing of years. To be effective a ceremony had to be performed exactly, and this involved the memorization of a precise series of sometimes several dozen acts, songs, chants and prayers. As a man grew old his voice weakened, his gestures became less forceful, and he might even get his lines mixed up and harm his patient. Hence, when a di-yin became too old to minister decisively, he might if he wished confide his ritual to a younger man.[25]

The lightning shaman was the only one who always received his power directly from the source; he was believed to be the most powerful shaman of all. Grenville Goodwin, an authority on Apache religion, explains:

Men who have only traditional curing rites are sharply distinguished from those who have the lightning ceremony. The latter alone are spoken of as "holy" and are considered so, i.e., invested with supernatural power of high quality. They are addressed in prayer, just like sources of power, for protection against lightning, etc. People also pray with pollen to the shaman conducting a lightning ceremony.[26]

However the shaman attained his power, he took his responsibility seriously. If he did not please the spirit who granted the power, it could be withdrawn, and in extreme cases the spirit might wreak vengeance on the shaman or his family. In addition to this burden of responsibility, the power could also bring prestige and wealth.

Power Brings Duties and Compensation

Every aspect of Apache life was touched by the influence of a shaman. The shaman, depending on the requirements of his particular power, might perform ceremonies commemorating the individual's passage through life—the first haircut, the first moccasins, or the girl's puberty rite, for example. He might apply his magic to healing the sick, preparing for war, or conducting special events such as weddings. Countless occasions called for ceremony and prayer and the services of a shaman.

These services were not free. The shaman made a living by performing or presiding over the sacred ceremonies. The early Apache did not use money, and compensation for services was offered in the form of gifts. The Apache understood the relative value of gifts suitable for the various ceremonies, and would be embarrassed to offer less than was expected. Sometimes the price was as high as several ponies. However, many ceremonies could be performed in either a simple or elaborate version depending on the wealth and desires of the family.

The Girl's Puberty Rite

The most important and elaborate ceremony was the Nah-ih-es, the girl's puberty rite. Most families went all out on this occasion and provided the most elaborate celebration they could afford. This girl's puberty rite celebrated the girl's first menstrual flow and welcomed her into adulthood:

> The Nah-ih-es was so elaborate—and costly to the girl's family—that they might begin making preparations as early as a year before they expected her time to come. Extra food was preserved and set aside, and hints could be dropped to relatives who were slow to contribute their share. Gifts from members of the community unrelated to the family also started to arrive: the feasting was open to all, and anyone who wanted to come sent a present.[27]

The Nah-ih-es required elaborate preparation. Although details of the ceremony varied from group to group, a ceremonial tipi for the girl, a dwelling for the shaman, and ramadas for food preparation had to be built. A special buckskin ceremonial dress was made for the girl and other ritual items such as a dancing cane, a drinking tube made from a reed, and a scratching stick were prepared for her. The cane symbolized longevity and was used in the dancing. The stick and tube were tied together with a long strip of rawhide. For the duration of the ceremony and four days afterward the girl could drink only through the tube and touch her face only with the

Apache Risk All for Ceremony

Ceremonies and rituals were very important in Apache life, and the girl's puberty rite was perhaps the most important of all. In Eve Ball's book *Indeh*, Asa Daklugie explains that sometimes its performance took precedence even over safety.

"Ceremonials for the Maidens are the most sacred of all our religious rites, and in the old days they were observed individually when the girl reached maturity. No matter what the situation the rite was held, although sometimes the observance had to be shorter than the customary four days. Once, when my people left [the reservation at] San Carlos for their dash for Mexico, they got into the Stein's Peak range and stopped. They knew that the cavalry was after them, but when one of the mothers announced that her daughter had reached maturity, the band had to observe the puberty rite. Women were baking mescal when we were attacked from the north and west. Unknown to us, another troop led by Forsyth, was coming in from the east to cut us off from Mexico. We had a terrible time there in order to cover the flight of the women."

stick. Mails writes that "if she drank otherwise, she would develop unsightly facial hair. If she touched her face other than with the stick, her complexion would be marred."[28]

This ceremony usually lasted four days, but for the Mescalero Apache it could last for as long as eight days. For the duration of the ceremony, the girl was called White-Painted Woman and was believed to have the powers of that deity.

This was an important social as well as religious occasion and there was much dancing and celebration. The Ganh Dancers, who impersonated a group of mountain spirits called the Ganh, were well known in Apache ceremonial occasions as forces with the power to cure disease and dissipate evil. The Nah-ih-es was the only ceremony in which the Ganh danced simply to entertain the crowd and spread good luck. The ceremony also involved ceremonial bathing and sprinkling with pollen. As with most Apache ceremonies, most rituals were performed four times and offerings were made to the four directions. When this elaborate ceremony was over, the girl was considered a woman and was free to marry.

Spiritual Healing

In addition to officiating at ceremonies like the Nah-ih-es, the shaman was the family doctor. The healing shaman carried a medicine bag of herbal cures, amulets, and magical objects such as turquoise and green malachite gemstones. These elaborately fringed and beaded bags were essential to the shaman, but he often preferred other healing methods.

The Apache believed that many illnesses were the result of affronts to the powers. Illness could be brought on by offending Owl, Coyote, or other spirits. It could also result from witchcraft or the malicious acts of ghosts. Shamans resorted to their stock of herbs on occasion, but they believed that illness caused by supernatural forces could best be treated by dances, chants, and rituals. Thomas Mails describes the typical healing process:

When a man was taken sick the medicine men took charge of the case, and the clansmen and friends of the patient were called upon to supply the fire and assist in the chorus. The only musical instrument employed was a flat rawhide drum or a pot drum nearly always improvised from an iron camp kettle, partially filled with water and covered with a piece of well-soaped cloth drawn as tight as possible. The Apache drumstick was a stick curved into a circle at one end; the stroke was not made perpendicular to the surface, but from one side to the other. Bourke states that in the

The Ganh Dancers, who impersonated dead mountain spirits, were believed to possess the power to cure diseases and ward off evil.

Various plants and roots, such as the yucca (pictured), were used by the Apache for medicinal purposes.

Apache view, all bodily disorders and ailments were attributed to evil spirits who must be expelled or placated. When there was only one person ill, the ritual consisted of singing and drumming exclusively, but dancing was added in all cases where an epidemic was raging or might spread in the tribe.[29]

Herbalism

According to Haley, the Apache did not think all illness was caused by the spirit world. Some illnesses were of natural causes and could be treated by the patient, his family, an herbalist, or a di-yin for healing. He relates the Apache belief in the power of plants: "When Yusn set up the world, he created all the plants at the same time. He gave all of them a purpose—not just the ones that are good to eat. Lots of them are good for medicine. Nothing is wasted! That's how they say it is."[30]

Apache women were well versed in the use of herbal remedies. They learned by trial and error and passed their knowledge on to the next generation. Kimberly Moore Buchanan, who teaches Texas history and is an expert on Apache women warriors, writes: "[Apache girls] were instructed in the medicinal values of plants and the nursing of minor ailments. A girl usually learned by observing her mother, grandmother, sister, or another older woman."[31] Over the years they developed a vast store of knowledge about the plants of the area and their medicinal value. Though the value of many remedies might have been primarily psychological, others were medically sound. A modern study reports some of the remedies used to treat common childhood ailments:

Facial blemishes were treated either with a mixture of ground moss and mushrooms or with a powder made from the prickly pear cactus. For an earache, Apache mothers rubbed the aural cavity with otter grease. A robin's egg mixed in water was said to help croup, boiled pennyroyal plant was given for fever. A child who exhibited signs of stomach distress might be fed the droop of a wild turkey, ground up and mixed with warm water. The Apache considered fearfulness no less an illness than a sore throat. One remedy to cure timidity was to give the child a drink made from herbs and the brain and eye of a woodhouse jay; another was to envelop the shy youth in the smoke of a burning stalk of bear grass.[32]

The Apache had a remarkable mastery of primitive medicine, but they lived a difficult life in a harsh environment and death was never far from their door.

He Who Has Gone

The Apache had a great respect for ghosts and did not like to speak of death. The words *dead* or *death* were seldom used. A deceased person was simply referred to as "He who has gone."

When an Apache died, family members prepared the body by washing it and dressing it in the person's best clothing. Sometimes they painted the face. It was important for the person to begin his journey to the afterlife looking his best. The body and a few prized possessions were taken into the desert

Ancient Remedies Are Gaining New Respect

Cherokee writer Gregg Howard criticizes modern man for putting insufficient faith in the medical lore of the early Native Americans in his on–line article "A Medical Conundrum."

"It's hard for us to believe that ancient peoples knew more about their world than we know about ours. We think, or we presume, that our knowledge has not only caught up with theirs but surpasses it. And yet, those primitive peoples may have known more about healing and preventing disease than we give them credit for. Their medicine was a combination of faith, blind luck and relying on the good earth—

relying on what was there. What nature provided was all there was. There was no corner drugstore, no medical specialist.

Yet, they knew what would keep them from getting sick and what potions would ease the pains of snake bite and rheumatism and child birth . . . what would heal the wounds of arrows and gunshots and other scars of battles in daily living.

Centuries of trial and error taught them what leaves and herbs and roots and smoke and heat and faith could do. They knew what could cure them and what could kill them. It was natural healing. And now, centuries later, the world is returning to it."[11]

or mountains for burial. As the funeral procession passed by, relatives joined in crying and wailing and other people politely looked away. Often the deceased person's favorite horse was killed, so that he could ride it to the Happy Place.

Geronimo, a Chiracahua Apache, describes his father's death:

> When I was but a small boy my father died, after having been sick for some time. When he passed away, carefully the watchers closed his eyes, then they arrayed him in his best clothes, painted his face afresh, wrapped a rich blanket around him, saddled his favorite horse, bore his arms in front of him, and led his horse behind, repeating in wailing tones his deeds of valor as they carried his body to a cove in the mountain. Then they slew his horses, and we gave away all of his other property, as was customary in our tribe, after which his body was deposited in the cave, his arms beside him. His grave is hidden by piles of stone. Wrapped in splendor he lies in seclusion, and the winds in the pines sing a low requiem over the dead warrior.[33]

Eve Ball studied the Apache in the 1950s. She gained the trust and friendship of Asa Daklugie, son of Chief Juh and nephew of Geronimo. She recorded many interviews with Daklugie and others. He talked to her about his people's beliefs about death and the afterlife:

> Our people believe in communication with their loved ones who have gone before them. If they speak in Apache the name of one who is dead, they summon the ghost of that person to them. This person might be hunting, or gambling, or sleeping [in the Happy Place] and not want to come, but he must. In our Happy Place we live just as we do here. Gambling is one of our favorite pastimes, so why not gamble in the Cloud Land [Happy Place]?
>
> In our Happy Place, we are to have bodies such as we have on earth, but they will never wear out, tire, or know hunger. Your book [the Bible] says that in your Heaven there will be no marrying nor giving in marriage. That may be the white man's idea of Paradise, but it isn't Mr. Apache's.

Daklugie adds a note of irony to his description of the Happy Place:

> We thought that even White Eyes might eventually be admitted to the Happy Place. Of course that'll never be done now, not with Geronimo there. If even one got in, the first thing we'd know surveyors would be invading and farmers stringing barbed wire over the place.[34]

Religion and spirituality may have been the guiding light of Apache culture, but conflict became its driving force and conflict would define their reputation in the white man's world.

Chapter 4

Building Toward a Life of Conflict

The Apache did not arrive in the Southwest as a conquering army bent on taking the land and its riches for themselves. They came in small groups seeking good hunting grounds and fresh water. They had no concept of land ownership and they measured wealth by a person's generosity to others in the group. Early tribes built friendly trading relations with some of the other native peoples such as the Yavapai.

Resources were limited, however, and the Apache could not always trade for the things they needed. Sometimes they stole from their neighbors. Sometimes the neighbors stole from them. It was a lifestyle marked by growing enmity among the people of the Southwest. The traditional enemies of the Apache included the Pima, the Maricopa, the Havasupai and the Walapai, and especially the Mexicans living to the south.

The exact causes of the growing animosity between the Apache and the other native peoples are unclear. But Thomas Mails points out that hostility does have

some advantages: "While with a friend one could only exchange gifts, an enemy became an economic source of some magnitude; enemies were desirable."[35] In other words, stealing from a friend was wrong, but stealing from an enemy was perfectly acceptable. So having many enemies created a valuable resource. On occasion serious battles erupted, but for the most part the hostile interactions consisted of raids for supplies.

Raids and Warfare

Raiding and warfare were two distinctly different things. A raid was a foray into an enemy camp to steal supplies and (in later days) horses and guns. Raids were usually undertaken at night by a handful of men. Their goal was to take what they wanted and disappear into the night with as little bloodshed as possible. Haley writes that

raiding was more an economic duty than a military adventure: admiration of skill in raiding stemmed not so

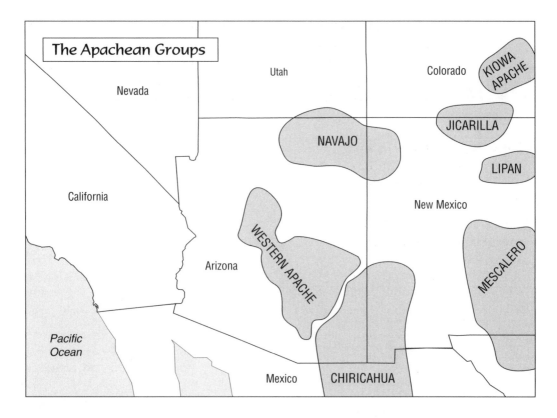

The Apachean Groups

Nevada

Utah

Colorado

KIOWA APACHE

JICARILLA

NAVAJO

LIPAN

California

New Mexico

WESTERN APACHE

Arizona

MESCALERO

Pacific Ocean

Mexico

CHIRICAHUA

much from a man being a good fighter as a good provider, and the few men who would not take part in raids were criticized not for cowardice but for laziness. A raiding party was small—as few as half a dozen men—and highly mobile. No dance was held beforehand to send them off, and no encounters with the enemy were sought.

. . . They harvested the peons [Mexican villagers] like a crop or renewable resource, taking what they needed in the way of stock and supplies, but always leaving enough behind for the people to rebuild.[36]

War parties were of a different nature, usually undertaken for revenge. A war party attacked with the intent to kill or capture as many of the enemy as possible. War parties were much larger than raiding parties, but by no means as large as the victims or the newspapers of the day reported.

The Apache prepared for war with fanfare and ceremony. A war dance lasted from one to several nights. The Chiricahua called the war dance the "Angry Dance." About the war dance Geronimo wrote:

After a council of the warriors had deliberated, and had prepared for the war path, the dance would be started. In this dance there is the usual singing led by the warriors and accompanied with the beating of the . . . [war drums], but the dancing is more violent, and yells and war whoops sometimes almost drown the music. Only warriors participated in this dance.[37]

For the ceremonial dancing the warriors dressed in their traditional breechcloths and moccasins, with the addition of ceremonial headgear. Apache warriors did not wear the elaborate feathered headdress usually associated with the stereotyped Indian warrior. Instead, most Apache wore a small hide war cap. These caps were often beaded, painted, or decorated with eagle or turkey feathers. Some Apache, the Mescalero in particular, also wore elaborately decorated buckskin war shirts. War paint was a matter of individual choice, but a leader with supernatural power might paint his men as his power directed him. Mails reports that Geronimo marked his men on the forehead, the sides of the face and across the nose.

The strongest, most aggressive warriors (usually but not always the chiefs of the band) led the war parties. The infamous Geronimo was not a chief; he led because he was a fearless warrior and a powerful medicine man.

Being accepted as a warrior was a sign of manhood for a young man and teenagers looked forward eagerly to the day when they would join a war party. But first each one had to go through a strenuous hardening process.

San Juan, a Mescalero Apache chief, displays his ceremonial robe, spear, and shield.

The Novice Warrior

Preparation to become a warrior stretched from childhood through puberty. Thomas Mails provides some details:

When a Chiricahua boy reached puberty, the age at which the girl was elevated to woman hood by the puberty rite, he was still undergoing the training process. But unlike the girl, he was not permitted to move quickly from childhood to maturity. The duties allotted to the young woman could be graduated according to her strength. But a man had to confront the dangerous realities of warfare; the young man on a raid or war party had to cover the same distance and suffer the same hardships as the strongest member of the group.[38]

When he felt he was ready, at about the age of fifteen, the young man requested to join a raid or war party as a novice. Once accepted, he had to participate in four raids before he could become a full-fledged warrior. Before his first raid he was issued a novice war cap by a shaman. His war cap was similar to that worn by the warriors, but was understood to carry less power. The shaman also gave him a scratching stick and a drinking tube. While on a raid as a novitiate, he could not scratch his head with his fingers, nor allow water to touch his lips. Instead he had to use the tube and stick, which he carried tied together by a length of rawhide and attached to his belt.

A novice was not allowed to participate in the actual raiding or fighting. Instead he had to cook for the warriors, care for the horses, stand guard, gather firewood, and perform other chores around the camp. Even the food he was allowed to eat and the words he could speak were strictly regulated. Geronimo wrote of novice warriors: "On the first trip he will be given only very inferior food. With this he must be contented without murmuring. On none of the four trips is he allowed to select his food as the warriors do, but must eat such food as he is permitted to have."[39]

Sometimes the four necessary raids could be completed in a very short time, but raids were never undertaken just to give the novice experience, so in times of peace, this training could last a year or longer. Once the novice had successfully completed his four training raids, he was a full-fledged warrior and a grown man ready to take a wife and begin his life as an adult.

An Explosion of Wrath

War and raiding were always a part of Apache life, but not until the Spaniards came marching out of the south astride their huge "mystery dogs," with helmets and breastplates flashing in the sun, did the Apache begin to learn the real meaning of hatred and savagery. They learned quickly and well.

The Spanish had long since colonized vast regions farther south in Mexico. They had no qualms about claiming for Spain

Weapons

Before they acquired firearms the Apache used a variety of traditional weapons.

Bow and Arrow: For a bow a straight piece of wood without knots was selected and shaped into either a single or double arc and strung with deer sinew. The single arc bow was more common. Arrows had a shaft of hardwood or cane. One end sported three feathers to guide the arrow in flight. The arrow points were made of stone (such as white flint), trade metal, or self-hardened wood, and were usually tipped with poison concocted from such ingredients as insect poison, poisonous plants, and rotting deer blood and liver. Bows and arrows were carried in either a single-piece self-quiver, or in a separate quiver and bow case. Mountain lion skin was the preferred material, but other leathers were used as well.

War Club: The Apache war club usually consisted of a short wooden stick for a handle, and a round stone head. A single piece of cow's tail or hide was slipped or wrapped over the head and sewed with sinew.

Lance: Lances were made of sotol stalks and were usually eight or nine feet long; some were as long as twelve feet. They were a silent and formidable weapon in the hands of a capable warrior and were often used by war leaders to prove their bravery.

Knife: Apache knives were originally made of stone or bone and carried in rawhide cases slipped under the belt. Later the Apache traded for or stole metal blades.

Shield: Most shields were made of cowhide and sometimes painted or decorated with feathers. A shaman with weapon power was usually retained to make the shield, which was suspended from the arm by two straps.

Apache arrowheads and other weapons were made from stone, bone, or hardened wood.

The Spanish frequently enslaved and abused the native peoples they encountered in the New World.

lands already inhabited by native peoples, and taking those people as slaves. It was simply the way things were done. Eventually they began working their way north, following elusive fables of cities rich in gold and jewels. Their first contacts in this new territory were with the Pueblo, who had established stable and usually peaceful societies. They were not prepared to do battle with the Spanish. On July 7, 1540, the Spanish explorer Coronado attacked the seven hundred Zuni of Hawikuh Pueblo. The editors of *The European*

Challenge describe the appearance of the Spanish soldiers:

There were about 100 of them, pale complexioned and bearded, encased from waist to neck in a turtle-like shell of glittering metal; another carapace protected their heads. The strangers carried formidable spears and long, gleaming metal knives. The Indians had heard vaguely of another weapon: a heavy stick that flashed fire and thunder, and brought death at great distances. More awesome still, many of the white warriors traveled astride what a Zuni scout had described as "fierce, man-eating animals"—beasts so huge and swift that the earth trembled beneath their hoofs.[40]

The Zuni stood little chance. In less than an hour the Spanish defeated them and looted their storerooms, setting in motion a centuries-long cycle of unequal struggle, a disastrous conflict for the Zuni and their way of life.

Gradually all of the Pueblo bowed to the superior might of the Spanish and were subdued by these European conquerors. Not so the Apache. Their villages were raided and their people killed or kidnapped into slavery. But the Apache were nomadic people who lived in small groups unencumbered by permanent homes or planted fields. They could break camp and fade into the mountains at a

Before meeting the Apache, the Spanish had overrun and defeated all of the Southwest tribes they had encountered.

moment's notice and launch their own attacks from mountain strongholds. And once abused, they had an insatiable taste for vengeance.

Guns and Horses

The Apache had always been cunning and formidable warriors, but the Spanish gave them the means to become even more deadly on the battlefield: guns and horses. The value of horses was quickly seen in civilian life, and the added edge they gave the warrior was soon recognized as well. The speed of the horse allowed the Apache to attack and depart suddenly, as well as range much farther afield and attack new targets.

The power and noise of the Spanish guns also impressed the Apache at once, but firearms came more slowly into use than did horses. The Apache had no gunsmiths to maintain their stolen guns, and they had to depend on stolen ammunition since they had no way of producing it themselves. Even when they could steal adequate ammunition, equipping themselves with the early guns did not present

Women Warriors

Women usually played a supportive role in warfare, but occasionally a woman would become a warrior and participate in ambushes and attacks. The best-known woman warrior was Lozen, sister of Chief Victorio, famed for her horse-stealing skill and her ability to locate the enemy. However, the story most often told about Lozen demonstrates her compassion as well as her abilities as a warrior. The incident is described by David Roberts in *Once They Moved Like the Wind*.

"Lozen was riding with a young, pregnant Mescalero woman who abruptly went into labor. Without hesitation, Lozen gave the woman's horse and her own to another fleeing Chihenne and slipped on foot into the brush to hide with the soon–to–be–mother.

(Had the women retained their horses, the cavalry would have found them.)

Even as the soldiers rode by within earshot, Lozen delivered the baby in the underbrush. There followed a long ordeal of survival, as Lozen guided the woman and her infant back to the Mescalero reservation. During their weeks of hiding and furtive movement, Lozen performed one virtuoso feat after another. Twice she stole Mexican horses from under the noses of their owners, fleeing in a hail of bullets. She killed a longhorn steer with only a knife, so the women could eat, then turned the animal's stomach into a water jug. Finally she managed to kill a cavalryman and helped herself to his rifle, ammunition, and canteen."

much of an advantage. The guns of the day were cumbersome and reloading was slow. Mails writes, "Then too, it took about thirty seconds to patch-load, aim, and fire a musket or rifle, whereas in thirty seconds an Indian could shoot from eight to ten arrows. It was also true that the bow could kill over almost the same range as an early gun could manage."[41]

On horseback Apache war parties moved swiftly across the desert, striking and vanishing into the night before sleeping victims could react. They were soon out of control, the scourge of the Southwest. Unable to subdue the hard-fighting Apache through force, as they had the Pueblo, the Spanish resorted to more insidious methods, detailed by Haley in *Apaches*:

> The Spanish handling of the Apache question took on yet another new complexion with the installation of Bernardo de Galvez as governor of the Interior Provinces in 1786. . . . [He] advanced a new theory, clever from the Spanish point of view but diabolical in the eyes of many historians, that the Apaches might be more easily conquered by peace than by unremitting war. But what a peace: the plan provided for the issuance, after the cessation of hostilities, of firearms to the Apaches, but firearms of sufficient antiquity and poor repair that they would need constant tinkering by trained gunsmiths, which would render them useless in the event the Indians re-

turned to war. The Apaches were also to be issued as much liquor as they could hold, for they had acquired the same fondness for the Spaniard's aguardiente [any of several Spanish alcoholic beverages] that was the curse of other Indian tribes. Apaches kept in a bleary stupor would, it was hoped, be more easily broken to Spanish rule than when sober and sharp-witted, and with luck they would become so addicted to distilled spirits as to depend on the Spanish for their supply, thus rendering war additionally unpleasant if not unthinkable.[42]

Unbroken Apache Might

According to Haley, despite a few serious flare-ups, Galvez's plan was effective. However, the system of buying off the Apaches cost the Spanish treasury between $18,000 and $30,000 per year. After the Mexican Revolution ended in 1821, the territory was returned to the Mexicans, who could not afford the high price of maintaining peace by subsidizing the Apache, and hostilities began anew. Haley writes that "once they were back at war, the Mexicans discovered that Galvez's principal object, the breakdown of Apache might, had not been obtained. Not only were the Apaches not broken-down drunks, they were more than a match for about any force the Mexican Government could muster out against them."[43]

Timekeeping

Apache men often traveled long distances and were gone from home for extended periods of time. In *The People Called Apache,* Thomas Mails reports that they had several methods of keeping track of their time away from home:

"One method being that of colored beads on a string—groups of six white ones to represent the days of the week, separated by one black or other colored bead for each Sunday. This method gave rise to some confusion, for the Apache had been told that there were four weeks and four Sundays in each moon. Therefore, most warriors found that their own method of determining time by the appearance of the crescent moon was more satisfactory. Another Apache method of indicating the passage of time was that of drawing a horizontal line on a piece of paper and then placing along this line individual circles or straight lines to represent the full days which had passed. A broad, straight line was drawn for each Sunday, and a small crescent line for the beginning of each month."

These timekeeping methods reflect the influence of Europeans, since the early Apache did not have paper and the Apache religion did not set aside a particular day of the week for religious observance (thus, Sunday would have been a meaningless concept prior to the introduction of Christianity). Opler also recorded several timekeeping methods described by an Apache source in *An Apache Life-Way*:

"Suppose you had promised someone to be somewhere in a certain number of days. You'd have to start at the right time to get there. So every morning you would throw a stone in a certain place and keep count of them. In this way you would know when to start. Or you might do it with marks on a stick. I have heard of doing it with beads on a string too, but with less specific detail."

Within fifteen years the Apache had killed at least five thousand settlers and caused thousands more to flee. Travel outside of major towns was very dangerous and more than one hundred settlements had been abandoned. The Mexicans resorted to desperate means in their attempt to defeat the Apache. Historian David Roberts describes the resulting carnage:

Both northern Mexican states, Sonora in 1835 and Chihuahua in 1837, had enacted genocidal laws offering a bounty on every Apache scalp turned in, even those of women and children. As late as 1849, Chihuahua raised the price on an Apache man's scalp to 200 pesos (about $200), while the rate for a woman or child taken captive was set at 150 pesos. In that year alone, the Chihuahua government paid out 17,897 pesos to bounty hunters. But instead of controlling the Apaches, the lucre created a bloody chaos. Cynical hunters soon learned that the government could not tell an Apache scalp from that of a Comanche or a Tarahumara; they even killed Mexicans and cashed in their scalps.[44]

According to most authorities the Mexicans and North Americans took far more scalps than the Apache ever did. For an Apache, taking a scalp was the worst possible punishment for an enemy. They took scalps only occasionally and only in the cases of bitterest revenge. For a bounty hunter, on the other hand, scalping was the road to wealth.

Pindah-Lickoyee

By the early 1800s U.S. citizens, adventurers and settlers alike, began trickling into the territory. There was scattered early contact with the Apache, but initially their presence drew little Apache attention. The Apache called the Americans pindah-lickoyee, or white-eyed enemies, but accepted their presence with minimal hostility. One man is assigned a large share of blame for the atmosphere of dis-

trust and hatred that developed between the Apache and the pindahs. In the early 1820s James Johnson, an American, built a warm and friendly relationship with Chief Juan José, but the Mexican bounty was a temptation stronger than the bonds of friendship and honor:

> Johnson threw a large feast for the Indians, [Juan José and his band] and when he judged that they had had enough to drink, he invited them to help themselves to a large mound of trade goods he had piled up for them. The celebrating Indians took advantage of the offer, unaware that Johnson had concealed behind the stack of gifts a cannon charged with grapeshot and iron scrap. At Johnson's signal the gun was fired, with terrible effect, as Johnson himself pointed his pistol at the stunned chief and shot him dead. Johnson collected fat bounties for the effort, but the Indian war he started blazed unchecked for years.[45]

Johnson set the tone, and interactions between the Apache and the American adventurers, settlers, and soldiers who poured into the Southwest in increasing numbers continued to involve terrible acts of betrayal and retaliation.

Chapter 5

Enemies from the East

The nineteenth century found Anglo-Americans marching relentlessly westward, fulfilling the doctrine known as manifest destiny. This political doctrine reflected the deeply felt belief of Americans that it was their god-given right to expand their nation's territorial claims across the continent from sea to sea.

The Apache, on the other hand, did not believe that land could be owned by any entity, individual, or government. However, they asserted their god-given right to continue to use the land as their ancestors had done for many generations. This basic clash of ideologies combined with cultural misunderstanding, greed, and fear to create a fertile environment for the growth of mistrust and hatred.

The Contested Texas Territory

The United States gobbled up Apache lands in the American thrust toward the Pacific, giving little thought to the rights of the natives already making their homes in the newly acquired territory. Texas, home to many Apache, had been officially claimed by Mexico but declared its independence in 1836. In 1845 Texas was admitted to the Union as a state. Mexico wanted the vast

The nineteenth century found an ever-increasing number of settlers invading Apache territory.

territory back, and went to war with the United States in 1846. Two years later Mexico surrendered, and the war ended with the Treaty of Guadalupe-Hidalgo. Mexico ceded to the United States 500,000 square miles of territory, which included much of New Mexico and Arizona, the traditional homelands of many Apache bands. Five years later the Gadsden Purchase added an additional 45,000 square miles of Apacheria (the name designating traditional Apache lands) to the United States.

By this time gold had been discovered in California and the trickle of settlers and prospectors had turned into a flood. Plans were under way for a railroad to span the continent, and military forts and trading posts were cropping up along major routes to offer both supplies and protection to the travelers.

Initially the Apache were not greatly concerned. They had no quarrel with the pindahs and they appreciated the steady supply of goods to trade for or steal. They were not concerned with national borders,

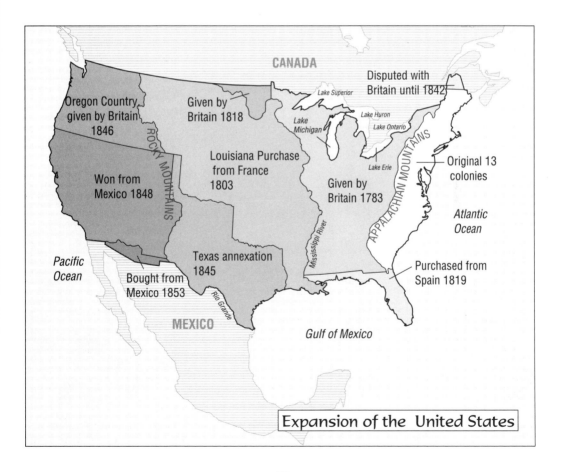

Expansion of the United States

which were just imaginary lines in the sand to them. They owed allegiance to neither the Mexican nor the U.S. government, and the land had been their home long before anyone else laid claim to it. However, they observed what was happening around them and soon learned that neither the U.S. nor Mexican armies would cross the invisible line separating those two countries.

The Apache took full advantage of the pindahs' policy of honoring borders by raiding homes and farms on one side of the border and fleeing to the safety of the other side. Eventually the United States and Mexico attempted to disrupt this convenient arrangement by means of a provision of the Guadalupe-Hidalgo treaty,

according to which the United States agreed to take steps to stop the Apache living on the U.S. side from raiding Mexican villages across the border. The North Americans also agreed to confiscate captives taken by the Apache and return them to Mexico.

The provision of the treaty relating to captives was almost impossible to enforce, but it was one of several factors that served to push the uneasy tolerance between the Apache and the Americans into open hostility. The Apache resented being harassed by the U.S. Army because of their raids into Mexico, and they were enraged by the seizure and return of their slaves to Mexico. Not only were slaves of

This 1884 photograph shows a group of Apache prisoners as they await their fate at Fort Bowie, Arizona.

great economic value to the Apache, but they were often accepted into the family and strong emotional bonds were formed. Adding to the tension was the fact that at least as many Apache were enslaved in Mexico and often treated with cruelty and forced into back-breaking labor. The treaty did not provide for the return of these individuals to their Apache homes.

Several incidents added fuel to the fire until the inflamed Apache raged out of control across the Southwest, viciously attacking settlements, wagon trains, and stage lines. Among these incidents three are remembered by the Apache even today with particular bitterness. One involved a well-known and powerful chief of the Chiracahua.

"Cut the Tent"

The Chiricahua called him Chies, which means "oak" in their language. He was named for the strength and quality of the great oak trees. The Anglos called him Cochise. According to Haley:

> Cochise was a fearsome warrior, a shrewd tactician, and a good provider—which meant a skilled raider—and his singular popularity with his people indicated that he was a strong and compassionate leader to his dependents. Though the Mexicans were terrified of him, he seems to have been well thought of by white men who knew him.[46]

Cochise was on good terms with the whites at the Butterfield Stage Station, near Fort Bowie in Arizona. Haley reports that he even accepted a contract to deliver wood to the station. All went well until the winter of 1860, when Apache raiders struck a nearby farm, stealing stock and capturing a twelve-year-old boy. The boy's stepfather accused Cochise's band of the kidnapping, even though they were known to be eighty miles away at the time. A detachment led by Lt. George Bascom set out from Fort Buchanan to investigate the incident.

Cochise was invited to Bascom's camp for a friendly talk. He arrived accompanied by an entourage of six of his followers (at least some of whom were relatives). Cochise went in the tent and was served coffee while the others waited outside. David Roberts describes the men who faced each other in the tent:

> The host, sitting tense and rigid inside the canvas army tent, his dark blue trousers dusty from a five days' march, was Second Lieutenant George N. Bascom. A full beard tapered to a V beneath his chin, failing to mute the earnest, callow face beneath. Heavy eyebrows overhung the bright stare of a zealot. A Kentuckian by birth, Bascom was about twenty-five years old; two years earlier, he had graduated from [the U.S. military academy at] West Point. Having served in Indian country for less than four months, he had just been handed his first opportunity to prove his mettle.

Cochise: Humbled but Proud

In September 1871 Chief Cochise, realizing that his men were being killed off and he was practically a prisoner in his own land, agreed to a meeting with General Gordon Granger. Captain Henry Stuart Turrill, who was present, later gave an account of the meeting in the speech "A Vanished Race of Aboriginal Founders" before the New York Society of Founders and Patriots of America on February 14, 1907. He quoted part of Cochise's speech as "the finest bit of Indian oratory that I have ever listened to."

"At last in my youth came the white man, under your people. Under the counsel of my father, who had for a very long time been the head of the Apaches, they were received with friendship. Soon their numbers increased and many passed through the country. I received favors from your people and did all that I could to return them, and we lived in peace. At last, your soldiers did me a very great wrong [the Bascom incident], and I and my people went to war with them. . . . I have destroyed many of your people, but where I have destroyed one white man, many have come to his place; where an Indian has been killed, there have been none to come in his place, so that the great people that welcomed you with acts of kindness to this land are now but a feeble band that fly before your soldiers as the deer before the hunter. . . . I have come to you not from my love for you or for your great father in Washington, or from any regard for him or his wishes, but as a conquered chief to try to save alive the few people that still remain to me. I am the last of my family."

An artist's rendition of the famous Apache chief Cochise.

His guest, . . . was twice the lieutenant's age. Tall for an Apache at five feet ten inches, he bore his taut-muscled 175 pounds with formal dignity. His dark black hair hung to his shoulders. From each ear dangled three large brass rings. A sharply bridged nose, high cheekbones, and a high forehead accented the gravity of his countenance. He never smiled.[47]

Bascom accused Cochise of kidnapping the boy. He dismissed the chief's denial and his offer to help find the kidnappers and negotiate the return of the boy. When he told the chief that he and his entourage would be held prisoner until the boy was returned, Cochise drew a hidden knife, slashed the side of the tent, and escaped. He ran alone into the mountains, with his six followers still held by the soldiers.

What happened over the next few days is the subject of contradictory accounts. In the end, however, Bascom's forces killed the Apache hostages. This incident, known in Apache folklore as "Cut the Tent," unleashed a fury in Cochise and his band that would leave an indelible mark on the history of the American West. Haley writes:

By one scholarly estimate, for two months after the Bascom affair the avenging Indians killed an average of twenty white people every week. Another opinion was that the ten long years of his [Cochise's] hostility cost approximately five thousand lives in raids and battles, a retribution so ter-

rible that his earlier [favorable] reputation was all but forgotten.[48]

Cochise was not the only chief to fall prey to the soldiers' trickery. His father-in-law, Mangas Coloradas, was one of the greatest of Apache chiefs. He was known to be a wise and reasonable man. The treachery that Cochise suffered at the hands of the Anglos pales in comparison to the treatment of Mangas Coloradas. His death in an incident known in Apache folklore as "the Black Pot" was a never-to-be-forgotten affront to all Apache.

The Black Pot

In the early days of his interaction with the Anglo-Americans, Mangas Coloradas was friendly and open and expressed the desire to live in peace with his white neighbors. A succession of insulting incidents transformed him into a revenge-crazed warrior who terrorized the region. Mangas once approached a group of prospectors with the suggestion that they could find much richer ore south of the border. Perhaps Mangas was sincere, or perhaps he hoped to peacefully encourage the miners to move on. Whatever his intention, the miners suspected a trick. They took him captive, tied him to a post, and severely beat him. Far more important than his physical injuries was the insult of such treatment of an important chief. Mangas vowed revenge and began a long career of brutal attacks on wagon trains, mail carriages, and settlements. His vendetta continued for many years, until his life ended in the final and most terrible insult that could be afforded an Apache.

Warriors Still

American Indians have defended their new government as valiantly as they did their homelands. More than ten thousand Indians served in the U.S. military during World War I. In World War II as many as forty thousand went to war out of a population of four hundred thousand. The proportion of Native Americans serving in Vietnam was significantly higher than their proportion in the general population.

In World War I Indians were not set apart in all-Indian units, but most were concentrated in outfits drawn from the National Guard of states with large Indian populations. And officers of those units sometimes grouped Indians together for special duties in the belief that they had natural gifts, such as an affinity for tracking or a talent for marksmanship.

However valid those assumptions, Indian soldiers did have one valuable and unique attribute: Their native languages are completely unrelated to English or any other European language, hence were impenetrable to German code breakers. Indian code talkers speaking by telephone easily confounded German eavesdroppers who had tapped Allied lines.

At nearly seventy, Mangas was still an able leader and formidable opponent. He was likely tired, however, and accepted an invitation to an army camp to discuss plans for peace. The invitation turned out to be a setup. The old chief was captured, beaten, burned with heated bayonets, and finally shot to death. Before dumping his body into a shallow grave, the soldiers scalped and beheaded him. His head was boiled in a black pot and the skull sent to the east for study. David Roberts writes:

The Apaches . . . waited and waited, but no word came to them. . . . Eventually . . . vague news of Mangas's martyrdom filtered back to his people. Somehow the news contained the information that the soldiers had boiled Mangas's severed head in a big black pot.

This revelation deeply stirred the Chiricahua sense of horror. Apaches believed that a person traveled in the afterlife in the physical state in which he had died. The Chiricahuas pictured their great chief wandering headless through eternity.

Many years later, Geronimo would say that the betrayal and murder of Mangas Coloradas was "perhaps the greatest wrong ever done to the Indians."[49]

As terrible as the death of Mangas Coloradas was, some point to another incident as an even greater example of man's inhumanity to man. Roberts writes, "White men in Arizona had performed atrocities against the Apaches before. But the Camp Grant massacre went beyond all previous bounds of wanton slaughter. Sixty-seven years later, a historian would call it 'the blackest page in the Anglo-Saxon records of Arizona.'"[50]

The Camp Grant Massacre

In February 1871 Camp Grant, fifty-five miles north of Tucson, was under the command of Lieutenant Royal Whitman. David Roberts notes this officer's unique character: "Under the most trying circumstances, he would prove to be one of those rare frontier figures, a military man who felt deep compassion for the Apaches. These qualities would cost him dearly in the public eye."[51]

A group of Apache of the Aravaipa band were living near Camp Grant in conditions of extreme poverty. Whitman did not have the authority to negotiate a truce with the Indians on his own, but he offered them food and protection while he waited for word from his superiors. Chief Eskiminzin and his people set up camp nearby. One night while most of the men were away on a hunting trip the camp was attacked by a group of vigilantes from Tucson. Between 125 and 144 Indians, mostly women and children, were brutally murdered as they slept. Many were first raped, and most were mutilated. Twenty-eight young children were kidnapped and sold into slavery.

Whitman wrote in his official report:

Many of the men, whose families had all been killed . . . were obliged to turn away, unable to speak, and too proud to show their grief. The women whose children had been killed or stolen were convulsed with grief, and looked to me appealingly, as though I was their last hope on earth.[52]

Local newspapers applauded the massacre, but President Ulysses S. Grant denounced it as murder and announced that he would put the whole territory under martial law if the guilty parties were not

President Ulysses S. Grant condemned the Camp Grant Massacre as murder.

General George Crook was one of the few Americans who earned the respect of the Apache.

apprehended and tried. Eventually more than one hundred people were indicted and tried. The trial lasted five days, and the jury deliberated for nineteen minutes before returning a not-guilty verdict for all. Today Oury Park in Tucson commemorates William S. Oury, the pioneer who organized and led the attack.

The other parties in this incident did not fare as well. Trumped-up trivial charges were used to discredit Lieutenant Whitman. He took an early pension and left the military. And Chief Eskiminzin, a man who sought peace for his people, in his despair dealt a fatal blow to that hope

for peace. According to David Roberts:

> Perhaps the most tragic deed in the aftermath of the massacre came at the hands of Eskiminzin. Near the end of May 1871, he visited a rancher on the San Pedro who was his closest white friend. Many times Eskiminzin had stopped here for a meal, and now the rancher invited him once more to dinner. The Aravaipa chief ate his friend's dinner, drank his coffee, then pulled out a gun and shot him dead.

Years later, Eskiminzin explained his act to an army scout. "I did it," the chief said, "to teach my people that there must be no friendship between them and the white men. Anyone can kill an enemy, but it takes a strong man to kill a friend."[53]

Too Little Goodwill, Too Many Misunderstandings

The Apache found little friendship or support in the remote government in Washington. Official policy varied from administration to administration, but usually Native Americans were relegated to the status of pests—a dangerous nuisance on U.S. soil. Whatever the government policy was at the moment, the relationship between Apache and American often came down to individual personalities. Both sides possessed men of peace and wisdom, but too often they were overshadowed by those driven by vengeance, greed, fear, and ignorance. Among the pindahs who earned the respect of the Apache were John P. Clum, John C. Cremony, General George Crook, and Royal Whitman. The understanding and friendship offered by these men and others like them never overcame the impact of those seeking glory or wealth, or those who simply lacked the wisdom to try to understand a different culture.

Many misunderstandings came from the failure of both sides to understand fully each other's policies or personalities. The Americans were accustomed to a hierarchy of government with a central seat of power in Washington. They did not grasp the significance of the Apache form of government—or lack of it. The seat of power for the Apache was the family, then the extended family and bands— groups loosely joined together for protection and socializing. The strength and power of the band depended on the ability of the chief to lead his people. No man was bound by the decisions of the chief. It was unheard of for the chiefs of a huge Apache nation to come together to powwow and make decisions for all their people. The federation type of government did not exist among the Apache bands.

The Americans never really understood that a treaty signed with Cochise,

for example, had nothing to do with all Apache and might not even apply to all Chiracahua Apache. The treaty was binding only on Cochise and those under his direct control—and any who disagreed with their chief's decisions could leave and join another band. The Americans often accused the Indians of breaking treaties, but in reality the supposed breaches usually involved a different band of Indians who had not signed the treaty in question.

The American government often took a cavalier attitude toward its treaties with indigenous peoples, and their commitments were seldom met. However, sometimes the fault did not lie with the government, but with the individual negotiating the treaty.

Misunderstandings led to hundreds of skirmishes between the Apache and the U.S. Army.

Negotiators often made promises of a happy life on traditional hunting grounds, but they had no authorization from Washington to grant these promises. Washington in fact intended to consolidate the Apache into a few controlled areas called reservations.

The End of the Apache Life-Way

The first Apache reservation, the Ojo Caliente reserve, was established in about 1870 and temporarily allowed the Eastern Chiricahua to remain in familiar territory.

Geronimo: Adapting to the Times

After his surrender Geronimo proved that he was still a determined survivor against all odds. Most of his people were shipped to a prison in St. Augustine, Florida, but Geronimo and a small group of warriors were imprisoned at Fort Pickens near Pensacola.

The inmates soon became a popular tourist attraction. Railroads sponsored excursions to Pensacola and tourist boats made regular trips to the island fortress where the "wild savages" were on display. The wily old warrior's raids on the Anglos took a new form: He signed autographs and allowed his picture to be taken—for a fee, of course. He also accepted gifts and sold small personal items.

Eventually the Apache were moved out of Fort Marion in St. Augustine and some family members, including three of Geronimo's wives, were sent to Fort Pickens. The occasion brought on a major tourist event, billed as the Grand Indian War Dance, which drew an estimated five hundred spectators.

In 1894 Geronimo and his people were moved to Fort Sill in Oklahoma, where he continued to be popular with tourists. He would sell his hat and the buttons of his coat, then select another hat from his stock and sew new buttons on the coat in preparation for the next transaction. The Time-Life book *The Reservations* describes Geronimo's 1904 trip to the world's fair in St. Louis to participate in the Native American exhibit:

[He] was loath to leave internment in Oklahoma to attend the fair. But once there, he was happy to make "plenty of money—more than I had ever owned before"—by selling his pictures and autograph. He was amazed by a magician who seemed to run a sword through a woman without injuring her. And he rode on a Ferris wheel: "I was scared," the old warrior said.

Geronimo died, still a prisoner of war, in 1909 in Lawton, Oklahoma. The cell where he was held at Fort Sill is still a tourist attraction.

One by one the Apache bands gave up the struggle and were forced onto the reservations. Finally only one remained. The fearless warrior Geronimo, still filled with the lust for vengeance, fought on against incredible odds. As many as five thousand U.S. soldiers and twenty-five hundred Mexican troops were engaged in the effort to locate and finally defeat Geronimo's band. At the end, the Apache leader commanded approximately thirty-four men, women, and children.

Geronimo

Geronimo was a powerful medicine man who believed that his war powers protected him from harm on the battlefield. His belief in his invincibility and his lust to avenge the death of his first wife and children (killed by Mexican troops) lent particular fearlessness and viciousness to his attacks on Mexicans and Americans. His daring and the savagery of his attacks drew sensational attention from the press and helped to build his reputation as the greatest of Apache leaders. In truth his band was small and he made many enemies among his own people. He never ruled with the wisdom and compassion of leaders such as Mangas Coloradas, Juh, Victorio, or Cochise. Many resented the unfavorable attention his continued warlike behavior brought to all Apache as they attempted to build a new life of peace.

Finally, Geronimo faced the inevitable and surrendered to General Nelson A. Miles on September 5, 1886. The groundwork for

Geronimo came to be feared as the most savage and dangerous Apache warrior.

the surrender had been laid by General Crook. Washington had demanded an unconditional surrender, but both Crook and Miles had made promises to the Apache that went well beyond their negotiating authority. Records are not clear as to exactly what the Apache were promised, but Geronimo seems to have believed that his people would be incarcerated briefly and then given a reservation of their own. Instead they faced a long imprisonment a continent away, in the unaccustomed humidity of Florida. Many sickened and died before the remnants were finally moved to Fort Sill in Oklahoma.

"Once I moved about like the wind," Geronimo said. "Now I surrender to you and that is all."[54]

Chapter 6

A New Life-Way

With the surrender of Geronimo peace came to the Southwest, but not to the Apache spirit. It was the end of the traditional life-way of a proud people, and the end was filled with broken promises, suffering, and indignity.

Although Geronimo's surrender in 1886 symbolizes the end of the Indian wars, the actual end of hostilities was not abrupt. Long before that time most of the Apache people and other American Indians had signed treaties with the U.S. government and were relocated to reservations. In exchange for signing a treaty the Indians were usually promised a large parcel of land in their traditional hunting grounds where they could live and hunt in peace. These reservations were open lands, not prisons enforced by walls or fences, so from time to time small bands left to participate in raids, or even to join war parties against the soldiers or settlers. For many, especially the young warriors, the transition to a sedentary life of dependency did not happen overnight but was a gradual process.

In reality the land set aside as reservations was seldom adequate for the needs of the people, offering little game and unsuitable for agriculture. Sometimes tribes were forced to leave their homeland and travel long distances to unfamiliar territory. Enemy tribes were sometimes crowded together on one reservation.

An old Lakota Sioux warrior summed up three centuries of relations between the white man and the Indian: "They made us many promises, more than I can remember," the man said, "but they kept but one. They promised to take our land, and they took it."[55]

Asa Daklugie described to Eve Ball the land set aside at San Carlos for a reservation:

San Carlos! That was the worst place in all the great territory stolen from the Apaches. If anybody had ever lived there permanently, no Apache knew of it. Where there is no grass there is no game. Nearly all of the vegetation was cacti; and though in season a little cactus fruit was produced, the rest of the year food was lacking. The heat was terrible. The insects were terrible. The water was terrible.[56]

A display at the San Carlos Apache Cultural Center describes the transition to reservation life:

As part of life on the reservation we became dependent on the handouts issued to us by the government of the United States. Often the rations failed to meet our basic needs, during the early reservation years food and supplies promised by the government were often sold off by dishonest Indian Agents, leaving us with shortages of food, cloth, or wood for cooking and warming our homes. In desperation our people left the reservation to hunt, gather plants and raid in traditional ways. These forays to relieve our poverty were commonly referred to as "outbreaks" in the local press. We were branded criminals in the struggle to maintain our dignity.[57]

Distribution of goods to the reservations presented lucrative opportunities to unscrupulous Indian agents. They accepted kickbacks from contractors and handed out shoes with paper soles, bags of grain containing less than the marked weight, and other shoddy products. One agent on

Many Apache had difficulty adjusting to a sedentary lifestyle on a reservation.

Early Reservations: A Long Road to Citizenship

The concept of confining Indians to small enclaves of land where they could be more easily controlled did not originate in the Southwest, but on the East Coast in the early 1600s. The exact nature of these Indian communities varied with the times and locations, but in most cases the European settlers and later the U.S. government made promises they would make little effort to keep.

In 1924 Congress formally conferred citizenship on all American Indians; however, the gesture was mostly empty. States could set their own voting qualifications, so citizenship did not even bring the right to vote. Not until 1948 could Indians vote in every state.

A group of Apache waits for the scheduled distribution of beef at the San Carlos Reservation.

the Apache reservation at San Carlos spent his time working on his private mining business; another stocked his ranch with government cattle. Corruption on and around the Indian reservations was so widespread that Civil War hero and Indian fighter General William T. Sherman described a reservation as "a parcel of land set aside for Indians, surrounded by thieves."[58]

When the meager rations did reach the Apache, they filled their stomachs—but not their need for self-reliance, independence, and dignity. People who had spent their time providing food and shelter for their families now found their hands idle with little to do but wait for the next government handout.

Government Responsibilities

With the Indians on reservations, the government in Washington assumed a responsibility to protect, supervise, and "civilize" them. The process often frustrated both sides. Government officials made little attempt to adapt their approach to native culture, and the Apache were angered and confused by the forced changes in their lifestyle. For example, the jobs that were available were often types of labor that were demeaning to Apache men. Some Apache tribes saw farming as women's work and the men were offended when they were expected to till the soil. Many Apache on reservations reacted to the baffling new life by turning to alcohol and too many saw suicide as a way out of an intolerable situation.

In the early days of reservations the government's good intentions toward the Indians were often misguided, and some official policies were in reality intended to encourage the white community to be more accepting of the idea of living near the "wild savages." But bored, unhappy Indians confined to a reservation made the settlers nervous, so they set out with missionary zeal to civilize them by turning them into versions of themselves. Surely some sincerely believed that they were doing what was best for the people on the reservations, but they defined "best" by European standards. The Apache had to wear European-style clothing, cut their hair, learn European standards of social behavior, and adopt the Christian religion. The government recognized that the easiest way to effect sweeping cultural changes was through the children, and focused much effort on the younger generation.

Boarding Schools

Many Apache children were taken away from their parents and sent away to boarding schools such as the Carlisle Indian Industrial School in Carlisle, Pennsylvania. These schools taught the Indian children English and math and some basic vocational skills. However, according to Richard Henry Pratt, founder of Carlisle School, the main goal of the school was to

Many people saw the government's handling of Indian affairs as ineffective, as depicted in this political cartoon.

This 1879 photograph of the Carlisle Indian School in Pennsylvania shows a group of Indian youth immediately after their arrival.

"kill the Indian and save the man."[59] He meant that the cultural heritage that gave the Indian child his identity should be stripped away and replaced with a new culture—that of the white man.

The attempt to "kill the Indian" began the day the children arrived at Carlisle. They were first photographed in their tribal garb and hairstyles. Before-and-after photos would be used to document the remarkable change that the school was expected to effect in the children. After the photographs, their hair was cut and their traditional clothing and possessions were destroyed. A former student wrote, "Our belongings were taken from us, even the little medicine bags

our mothers had given us to protect us from harm. Everything was placed in a heap and set afire."[60] (The destruction of a medicine bag was believed to bring serious bad luck.) After being deprived of their few personal possessions the students were issued new European-style clothing and a new identity. Eve Ball describes the admission process:

> At Carlisle, the school for Indians near Harrisburg, Pennsylvania, the newly arrived Apache boys and girls were lined up and given names, arbitrarily selected, alphabetically down the lines. "Asa" Daklugie was at the head of the boys' line when names were dispensed to his group. Also,

the age of each was estimated and a specific date of birth—day, month, and year—was arbitrarily assigned to each.[61]

The plan to "kill the Indian" seldom worked. Tribal beliefs and loyalty remained strong. Some Apache leaders even chose to send their children to the white man's school to improve their potential as leaders of their people. For example, Asa Daklugie attended the school because his uncle Geronimo chose to send him to Carlisle. Daklugie explains why:

Not all selected were descended from chiefs, but they might be the leaders of the Apaches in the future—provided that there was any future. Without this training in the ways of the White Eyes our people could never compete with them. So it was necessary that those destined for leadership prepare themselves to cope with the enemy. I was to be trained to become the leader.[62]

There was some wisdom in Geronimo's decision to educate his nephew in the ways of the white man. Asa Daklugie spent eight years at Carlisle and returned home to be a leader of his people, but he never overcame his deep distrust of the white man. The Time-Life book *The Reservations* reports that many of the boarding-school students never quite fit into either society after their time at school. However, others used their education to take a leadership role as Geronimo had predicted: "A new generation

Some Apache leaders felt that the skills learned at the boarding schools (pictured) would someday be an asset in the struggle against the white man.

of leaders emerged at the tribal level as well as nationally. Boarding school graduates returning home armed with a mastery of the English language and an understanding of American political and legal institutions used their knowledge to try to right old wrongs."[63]

Although the schools taught the Apache children to understand the ways of the white man, few of them embraced this new lifestyle. Most were homesick and missed their families and tribal customs. They longed for the day they would be allowed to return to their families, but for many that day never came. They were buried at Carlisle School. They had no natural resistance to the white man's diseases and many became ill and died. Between

Apache Education

Formal schooling was unknown to the early Apache. Children learned the skills and traditions required for success in their culture from their parents. Their forced transition into a modern education system has not been easy. The boarding-school system was a failure, and eventually schools were built on or near the reservations, but the Apache still resented the required schooling as a disruption of their family life.

Schools were more readily accepted after the Indian Reorganization Act of 1934 allowed the reservation schools to begin teaching some aspects of Apache culture. In the 1950s and 1960s a stronger emphasis was placed on education on the reservations, and financial aid was made available and administered by an education committee of the tribal council. The committee purchases clothes and school supplies, and administers a college scholarship fund.

To bolster Native Americans' success in college, tribal community colleges such as the Haskell Indian Nations University and Southwestern Indian Polytechnic were established by the BIA. By 1997 almost twenty-five thousand students were enrolled in about thirty such colleges. Still, according to an on-line report on Apache education "[Apache students] have a hard time adjusting to life away from their families. Combined with the lack of strong Native American role models that students can look up to for motivation, the result is that Native American students have the worst college dropout rates in the United States."

Many students also face serious financial problems. More than 50 percent of those attending these colleges are single parents, and a shocking 85 percent live below the poverty level. In spite of increased emphasis on education only about 4 percent of American Indians ever complete a degree, and unemployment rates still range from 45 to 86 percent on reservations.

April 13 and November 7, 1886, thirty Apache youth died at Carlisle School.

The Bureau of Indian Affairs (BIA)

In addition to the attempts to remake the Indian children in the European mold, government officials were faced with management and administrative issues on the reservations. Administration of the reservations fell under the jurisdiction of the Bureau of Indian Affairs (BIA), which was established in 1824 as part of the War Department to handle Indian affairs.

Today more than 90 percent of BIA employees are Indian. Now a part of the Department of the Interior, the bureau administers and manages over 56 million acres of land held in trust by the United States for Indians. This responsibility includes developing forest lands, leasing mineral rights, directing agricultural programs, and protecting water and land rights.

The BIA also funds federal schools on reservations, provides health care, and offers housing assistance to Indians. Since the 1970s, American Indians have pushed for greater self-determination and less administration by the BIA.

Sovereignty and Indian Gaming

Sovereignty has various meanings. Dictionary definitions include "one possessing the supreme power and authority of the state," "supreme in power or authority," and "to govern without external control."

Most tribes consider themselves separate sovereign nations and would like to be treated as such by the federal government. But the question of whether or not they are sovereign nations, and if so exactly what that means, is a weighty one. It is an issue that has found its way to the Supreme Court on numerous occasions.

Three Supreme Court cases known collectively as the Marshall trilogy, after Chief Justice John Marshall, established a framework for determining Indian sovereignty. Although the principles established by the Marshall trilogy still guide the Court in questions of tribal sovereignty, the issue is often misunderstood and open to interpretation.

The question of sovereignty often comes into play when tribes desire to establish businesses that may not conform to state law. Apache and other Native Americans believe that as sovereign nations they should be independent from the state in which they are located, and that they should not be required to pay the taxes of that state. For example, many tribes, including several Apache tribes, have opened bingo halls and casinos that do not conform to the gambling laws of the state where they are located. To justify these actions, they cite the final case of the Marshall trilogy, *Worcester v. Georgia* (1832), in which the Court ruled that the laws of a state have no effect in Indian country. Thus states cannot extend their regulatory or taxing jurisdiction to reservations, apparently leaving the door wide open for gambling and state-tax-free cigarette sales, for example, on Indian land. The reservations must still abide by federal law, however, and some special laws have been enacted to address the issue. But many questions of tribal/state jurisdiction remain unclear.

In 1988 the Indian Gaming Regulatory Act was passed. The IGRA divides Indian gaming into three classifications and stipulates that in order to operate Class III games, which includes most casino-type games, the tribe must negotiate a compact with the state. The state is required by law to negotiate in good faith. It was a solution that left neither the Native Americans nor the states fully satisfied, and many questions are still unanswered.

Approximately one-third of American Indian tribes, including several Apache tribes, now operate gaming facilities of some type. Although only 5 percent of gaming revenues in the United States are derived from Indian gaming, tribes that operate gaming facilities believe that the gaming industry has had a strong and positive economic impact on their people. Casinos have brought new prosperity to several Apache tribes.

Reservations Today

Today Apache live both on and off reservations. They work as teachers, doctors, nurses, lawyers, firemen, telephone linemen, and all of the other vocations that

Indian gaming has benefited many tribes, including the Apache. By creating jobs, increasing revenues, and reducing welfare needs, casinos have brought prosperity to many Apache.

Members of the Mescalero Apache tribe perform the traditional Ganh Dance for a group of tourists in New Mexico.

make up a complex society. The reservations still suffer from high rates of unemployment, substance abuse, and other social problems. However, some of the reservations are prospering with flourishing industry and entertainment facilities.

For example, thirteen thousand White Mountain Apache tribe members live on the 1.6-million-acre Fort Apache Indian Reservation in east-central Arizona. The main sources of income on the reservation are livestock and businesses catering to tourists. Tribal members operate the Sunrise Ski Resort and the HonDah (which means welcome in Apache) Casino. They also attract tourists to their Culture Center for traditional dances, arts and crafts, and rodeos.

Some tribes see the natural curiosity and interest of non-natives as an opportunity for promoting understanding and generating income; others, however, are still distrustful of outside interests.

Changing Attitudes

Many Apache and other Native Americans are hesitant to share information about their tribe with non-natives, believing that their people have been too often misrepresented and misquoted. Alonzo Chalepah, cultural resource specialist for the Apache Tribe of Oklahoma, has compiled numerous oral history tapes, most of which focus on preserving the tribe's language. The tapes are available for tribal use only. Chalepah says that tribe members do not want to give away their "cultural identity markers"[64] because they have nothing else left.

Other Apache take a different view. Terry Ravey, a Mescalero Apache, is a teacher in Pensacola, Florida. He and his wife are artists and own a gallery in the historical district of Pensacola. Their art reflects their heritage and their sensitivity to the world around them. Ravey agrees that their heritage is all that remains of the old way of life, and he understands the hesitancy some of his people feel about sharing some aspects of their culture. However, he does not agree that it should all be hidden from the world. He feels that it has great value as an educational tool to promote cultural understanding. He willingly shares his memories of life near the Fort Grant reservation and enjoys showing his traditional clothing, medicine bags, and bows. Ravey says because his people have no written language they have relied on father telling son to preserve their heritage, which he does not fear losing because "the spirit [of the Apache people]

won't die because it is the truth, and a truth cannot die."[65]

Michael Darrow of the Fort Sill Apache Tribe also struggles to preserve his tribe's identity. He is reportedly the only remaining fluent speaker of his tribe's language. He is transcribing the tribe's only real language source, the Chiricahua-Mescalero Apache Texts. Ron Jackson writes in the *Sunday Oklahoman*:

> Tribal historian Michael Darrow battles against the odds daily in hopes of preserving the language of his people—descendents of legends such as Mangas Coloradas, Cochise and Geronimo. Those men once fought for freedom. Darrow fights for their words.
>
> "To me, this is pretty much all that remains of the wealth of the families in our tribe," Darrow, 42, said recently at the Fort Sill-Apache tribal headquarters north of Lawton. "We were once a prosperous nation with our own land and our own everything. And pretty much everything physical our people owned was taken away.
>
> "Our language is one of the few treasures we have remaining."[66]

Facing the Future

The Indian survived our open intention of wiping them out, and since the tide turned they have even weathered our good intentions toward them, which can be more deadly. —*John Steinbeck*

Over a century has passed since the surrender of Geronimo and the end of the Indian wars, yet the relationship between the Indian and the U.S. government continues to be characterized by misunderstanding and insensitivity. Official policy and public opinion have changed over time. For many years the Apache and other American Indians were seen as dangerous savages who needed to be civilized. Because the Apache called their god Ussen and believed in the supernatural power in all of the things around them, U.S. citizens saw them as heathens and believed that it was necessary to convert them to Christianity. Reformers believed that they would be much better off if they put their tribal beliefs and customs behind them and learned the ways of the conquerors. Sometimes

Today, many Apache are taking advantage of the numerous opportunities available to them.

they were viewed as ignorant and childlike wards of society, who had to be fed, clothed, and cared for.

The perspective of the 1970s, understanding to a fault, transformed the American Indian past and present into the noble savage. The Apache people and other Native Americans were viewed as wise sages who had suffered heroically and innocently at the hands of an unfeeling government. Yet like the narrow-minded, patronizing attitudes of earlier years, the more liberal view fails to paint a complete or accurate picture.

Today American Indians are coming to be seen as individuals, products of their environment and heritage. And although inequities still exist and questions about sovereignty and the future of the reservations remain unanswered, the Apache face the twenty-first century with pride in their ethnic background and move with renewed self-confidence into their place in the larger society.

Notes

Chapter 1: Adapting to a New Land

1. Editors of Time-Life Books, *People of the Desert*. Alexandria, VA: Time-Life Books, 1993, p. 140.
2. James L. Haley, *Apaches: A History and Culture Portrait*. Garden City, NY: Doubleday, 1981, p.11.
3. Thomas E. Mails, *The Mystic Warriors of the Plains*. New York: Marlowe, 1995, p. 17.
4. Morris Edward Opler, *An Apache Life-Way: The Economic, Social, and Religious Institutions of the Chiricahua Indians*. Lincoln: University of Nebraska Press, 1996, p. 385.
5. Quoted in Opler, *An Apache Life-Way*, p. 226.
6. Haley, *Apaches*, p. 122.

Chapter 2: Growing Up Apache

7. Quoted in Opler, *An Apache Life-Way*, p. 6.
8. Haley, *Apaches*, p. 124.
9. Quoted in Opler, *An Apache Life-Way*, p. 8.
10. Quoted in Opler, *An Apache Life-Way*, p. 11.
11. Haley, *Apaches*, p. 128.
12. Haley, *Apaches*, p. 127.
13. Quoted in Opler, *An Apache Life-Way*, p. 27.
14. Quoted in Opler, *An Apache Life-Way*, p. 35.

15. Editors of Time-Life Books, *People of the Desert*, p. 147.
16. Opler, *An Apache Life-Way*, p. 46.
17. Editors of Time-Life Books, *The Way of the Warrior*. Alexandria, VA: Time-Life Books, 1993, p. 42.
18. Editors of Time-Life Books, *People of the Desert*, p. 147.
19. Haley, *Apaches*, p. 144.

Chapter 3: The Power Was Everywhere

20. Gregg Howard, "The Medicine Man," *Native American Healing,* learnFREE, Inc., 1999, http://www.nativeamerican healing.com.
21. Quoted in Haley, *Apaches*, p. 14.
22. Quoted in Haley, *Apaches*, p. 14.
23. Quoted in Haley, *Apaches*, p. 63.
24. Quoted in Opler, *An Apache Life-Way*, p. 202.
25. Haley, *Apaches*, p. 64.
26. Quoted in William S. Lyon, *Encyclopedia of Native American Healing*. New York: W. W. Norton, 1996, p. 152.
27. Quoted in Haley, *Apaches*, p. 64.
28. Thomas E. Mails, *The People Called Apache*. Englewood Cliffs, NJ: Prentice-Hall, 1974, p. 74.
29. Mails, *The People Called Apache*, p. 144.
30. Quoted in Haley, *Apaches*, p. 76.
31. Kimberly Moore Buchanan, *Apache Women Warriors*. El Paso: University

of Texas, Texas Western Press, 1986, p. 14.

32. Editors of Time-Life Books, *Cycles of Life*. Alexandria, VA: Time-Life Books, 1994, p. 37.

33. Quoted in Peter Meindertsma et al., *Geronimo: His Own Story*, The American Revolution, an .HTML project, 1997, http://odur.let.rug.nl/~usa/B/geronimo/genoni3.htm.

34. Quoted in Eve Ball, *Indeh: An Apache Odyssey*. Norman: University of Oklahoma Press, 1988, p. 57.

Chapter 4: Building Toward a Life of Conflict

35. Mails, *The People Called Apache*, p. 28.

36. Haley, *Apaches*, p. 116.

37. Quoted in Meindertsma et al., *Geronimo*.

38. Mails, *The People Called Apache*, p. 260.

39. Quoted in Meindertsma et al. *Geronimo*.

40. Editors of Time-Life Books, *The European Challenge*. Alexandria, VA: Time-Life Books, p. 103.

41. Mails, *The People Called Apache*, p. 477.

42. Haley, *Apaches*, p. 39.

43. Haley, *Apaches*, p. 15.

44. David Roberts, *Once They Moved Like the Wind: Cochise, Geronimo, and the Apache Wars*. New York: Simon and Schuster, 1993, p. 108.

45. Haley, *Apaches*, p. 52.

Chapter 5: Enemies from the East

46. Haley, *Apaches*, p. 224.

47. Roberts, *Once They Moved Like the Wind*, p. 21.

48. Haley, *Apaches*, p. 228.

49. Roberts, *Once They Moved Like the Wind*, p. 42.

50. Roberts, *Once They Moved Like the Wind*, p. 74.

51. Roberts, *Once They Moved Like the Wind*, p. 68.

52. Quoted in Roberts, *Once They Moved Like the Wind*, p. 74.

53. Roberts, *Once They Moved Like the Wind*, p. 75.

54. Quoted in Roberts, *Once They Moved Like the Wind*, flyleaf.

Chapter 6: A New Life-Way

55. Quoted in Editors of Time-Life Books, *The Reservations*. Alexandria, VA: Time-Life Books, 1995, p. 45.

56. Quoted in Ball, *Indeh*, p. 37.

57. San Carlos Apache Cultural Center Website, http://www.carizona.com/super/attractions/san_carlos.html.

58. Quoted in Editors of Time-Life Books, *The Reservations*, p. 79.

59. Quoted in Editors of Time-Life Books, *The Reservations*, p. 6.

60. Quoted in Editors of Time-Life Books, *The Reservations*, p. 96.

61. Ball, *Indeh*, p. 13.

62. Quoted in Ball, *Indeh*, p. 135.

63. Editors of Time-Life Books, *The Reservations*, p. 142.

64. Alonzo Chalepah, Apache Tribe of Oklahoma, Interview, June 10, 1999.

65. Terry Ravey, Mescalero Apache, Interview with the author, Pensacola, Florida, June 2, 1999 and January 15, 2000.

66. Ron Jackson, "Apache Holdout, Historian Battles to Preserve Words His People Spoke," *Sunday Oklahoman*, June 6, 1999, p. 1.

Glossary

adobe: Sun-dried clay, or the brick made from such clay; buildings made from adobe, particularly the dwellings of the Pueblo Indians of the Southwest.

Apacheria: The area comprising most of Arizona and Mexico and parts of surrounding states that made up the traditional Apache homelands.

buckskin: A soft yellowish gray leather made of the hide of a deer or sometimes a sheep.

cross-cousin: A child of either sex of one's father's sister or mother's brother. This relationship was usually characterized by exchanging puns, pranks, and practical jokes. Cross-cousins were also used to arrange meetings between couples who were interested in each other, but too shy to make the approach themselves.

culture: The way of life of a group of people, including how they live, the tools they make, the ceremonies and rituals they practice, their arts, and how and what they think.

di-yin: Another name for a shaman or medicine man or woman. An Apache religious leader. Since the Apache had no written language, spellings vary: sometimes the plural is di-yins, but di-yin is also seen.

Ganh: In Apache mythology, Mountain Spirits sent by Ussen to help the People; they were the link to the high cosmos.

ha-dintin: Pollen from cattails, corn, or other plants; considered to have beneficial powers, it was used in many ceremonies and rituals.

manifest destiny: A nineteenth-century doctrine claiming continued territorial expansion of the United States as its obvious destiny.

pemmican: An Indian food, often carried by hunters and warriors, made of dried pulverized meat mixed with animal fat and sometimes dried berries.

pitch: A resin found in certain evergreen trees used by the Indians for waterproofing; also, a black sticky substance formed from tar.

Pueblo: A name, meaning town, that the Spanish gave to the many indigenous peoples who lived in villages of permanent adobe dwellings.

tipi: An Indian dwelling constructed of a cone-shaped frame of poles covered by animal skins.

rawhide: An untanned or only partially tanned animal hide.

reservation: Public land set aside for some special use.

shaman: Medicine man or woman.

sinew: An animal tendon used by the Apache as cord for tying.

tan: To change hide into leather by soaking in tannin or other chemical.

tribe: A group of people having a common language, a common name for themselves, and claiming a definite territory. Some tribes have some form of government, others have little or none.

For Further Reading

Neil Philip, ed., *Earth Always Endures: Native American Poems*. New York: Penguin Books, 1996. This selection of Native American poetry, beautifully illustrated with photographs by Edward S. Curtis, provides insights into the thoughts and way of life of Native Americans. Curtis, born in 1868, began photographing the changing Native American culture in 1898 and devoted the next thirty years to the project.

Lou Cuevas, *Apache Legends: Songs of the Wind Dancer*. Happy Camp, CA: Naturegraph, 1991. Delightful Apache legends originally related in song by Lou Cuevas's Apache grandfather. They tell about the origins of many familiar desert and prairie creatures that were important in the Apache worldview. They open windows to the soul of the Apache, and are a fun read as well.

Morris Edward Opler, *Myths and Tales of the Jicarilla Apache Indians*. New York: Dover, 1994. An entertaining and educational collection of Jicarilla Apache tales collected and edited by one of the foremost authorities on Apache culture.

Frederic Remington, *On the Apache Indian Reservations and Artist Wanderings Among the Cheyennes*. Palmer Lake, CO: Filter Press, 1974. This booklet reprints two of Remington's illustrated stories published in the *Century Magazine* issues of July and August 1889. The stories are an interesting read and Remington's beautiful drawings are well worth study.

Works Consulted

Books

Eve Ball, *Indeh: An Apache Odyssey*. Norman: University of Oklahoma Press, 1988. Ball interviewed over 150 American Indians and dozens of non-Indians to write this beautiful saga of Apache life. Much of the text centers around Chief Juh, based on information given by his son Asa Daklugie. According to Ball the Apache word *Indeh* means "the Dead," and is the term by which Apache, recognizing their fate, designated themselves. The book is a good read and gives the reader the opportunity to know the Apache as fellow humans.

Robert F. Berkhofer Jr., *The White Man's Indian*. New York: Knopf, 1978. Images of the American Indian from Columbus to the present.

John G. Bourke, *The Medicine Men of the Apache*. Glorieta, NM: Rio Grande Press, 1970. This study was first written as a paper for the Ninth Annual Report of the Bureau of Ethnology of the Smithsonian Institute for the years 1887–1888. Bourke based his report on many interviews and a sincere attempt to understand the beliefs of the Apache people.

Kimberly Moore Buchanan, *Apache Women Warriors*. El Paso: University of Texas, Texas Western Press, 1986. A study of the role that Apache women played outside the traditional woman's role. Includes participation in war parties alongside their husbands and, in the case of Lozen and a few others, their role as warriors independent of a husband.

Editors of Time-Life Books, *Cycles of Life*. Alexandria, VA: Time-Life Books, 1994. This book examines the life cycles, rites of passage, ceremonies, and lifestyles of Native Americans.

Editors of Time-Life Books, *The European Challenge*. Alexandria, VA: Time-Life Books, 1992. This book chronicles the interactions between Europeans and Native Americans.

Editors of Time-Life Books, *People of the Desert*. Alexandria, VA: Time-Life Books, 1993. An overview of the history and culture of the indigenous peoples of the American Southwest, including the Pueblo, Apache, and Navajo.

Editors of Time-Life Books, *The Reservations*. Alexandria, VA: Time-Life Books, 1995. An overview of the American Indian reservation system in the United States.

Editors of Time-Life Books, *Tribes of the Southern Plains*. Alexandria, VA: Time-Life Books, 1995. An overview of the history and culture of the indigenous peoples of the Southern Plains including the Apache of that area.

Editors of Time-Life Books, *The Way of the Warrior*. Alexandria, VA: Time-Life Books, 1993. This book examines the weapons and philosophy of warfare of the Native American people.

James L. Haley, *Apaches: A History and Culture Portrait*. Garden City, NY: Doubleday, 1981. A well-written and meticulously researched narrative of the culture and history of the Apache people. Haley relies heavily on Opler's earlier research, but expands his scope to include all of the Apache people rather than just the Chiricahua.

Bobby Lake-Thom, *Spirits of the Earth: A Guide to Native American Nature Symbols, Stories, and Ceremonies*. New York: Penguin Group, 1997. The details of Apache religious beliefs and those of other Native Americans vary, but the underlying system of belief is very similar. Bobby Lake-Thom draws on the experiences of people from many different tribes and summarizes the system of knowledge.

William S. Lyon, *Encyclopedia of Native American Healing.* New York: W. W. Norton, 1996. An alphabetical listing and explanation of hundreds of Native American words and healing practices. Lyon presents a wealth of information in an informative and readable style.

Thomas E. Mails, *The Mystic Warriors of the Plains*. New York: Marlowe, 1995. A detailed account of the life of the Plains Indians, beautifully and extensively illustrated with detailed line drawings by the author.

Thomas E. Mails, *The People Called Apache*. Englewood Cliffs, NJ: Prentice-Hall, 1974. A comprehensive look at Apache culture, beautifully illustrated with paintings and drawings by the author.

Morris Edward Opler, *An Apache Life-Way: The Economic, Social, and Religious Institutions of the Chiricahua Indians*. Lincoln: University of Nebraska Press, 1996. This book, based on dozens of in-depth interviews, is one of the most comprehensive studies available on Apache culture.

David Roberts, *Once They Moved Like the Wind: Cochise, Geronimo, and the Apache Wars*. New York: Simon and Schuster, 1993. This book is about the Chiricahua Apache who were the last holdouts in the Indian Wars. It is about the individuals involved, particularly Cochise and Geronimo.

Woodward B. Skinner, *Geronimo at Fort Pickens*. Pensacola, FL: Skinner Publications, 1981. This booklet describes the imprisonment of Geronimo and his people in Fort Pickens near Pensacola, Florida, where he was welcomed by the local population as a celebrity and a tourist attraction.

Internet Sources

Apache Education: The Preservation of a Culture, http://members. tripod.com/archaeology_man/education.htm.

Gregg Howard, "A Medical Conundrum," *Native American Healing*, learnFREE, Inc., 1999, http://www.nativeamerican healing.com.

Gregg Howard, "The Medicine Man," *Native American Healing*, learnFREE, Inc., 1999, http://www.nativeamericanhealing.com.

Peter Meindertsma et al., *Geronimo: His Own Story*, The American Revolution, an .HTML project, 1997, http://odur.let.rug.nl/~usa /B/geronimo/genoni3.htm.

Philip J. Prygoski, *From Marshall to Marshall, The Supreme Court's changing stance on tribal sovereignty*, http://www. abanet.org/genpractice/compleat/f95marshall.html.

Indian Gaming Regulatory Act (IGRA), http://www.sanmanuel. com/Igra.html.

San Carlos Apache Cultural Center Website, http://www.carizona.com/ super/attractions/san_carlos.html.

Through Apache Eyes, Purple Hawks Nest, http://www.geocities. com/RainForest/canopy/8494/quotes.html.

Periodicals

Alonzo Chalepah, Apache Tribe of Oklahoma, Interview, June 10, 1999.

Ron Jackson, "Apache Holdout, Historian Battles to Preserve Words His People Spoke," *Sunday Oklahoman*, June 6, 1999.

Terry Ravey, Mescalero Apache, Interview with the Author, Pensacola, Florida, June 2, 1999 and January 15, 2000.

Index

Picture Credits

Cover Photo: Peter Newark's Western Americana
Archive Photos, 19, 26, 30, 42
Arizona Historical Society, 60
© Carolyn A. McKeone/FPG, 79
Charles and Josette Lenars/Corbis, 41
E. O. Hoppé/Corbis, 16
© FPG International, 12, 23
© Jonathan A. Myers/FPG, 77
Library of Congress, 20, 37, 56, 63, 64, 67, 71
National Archives, 9, 27, 47, 49, 58, 69, 72, 73
North Wind Picture Archives, 8, 21, 38, 50, 51, 65, 70
Phil Schermeister/Corbis, 76

About the Author

Anne Ake edited an arts magazine for eight years, and with her daughter owned and published *Cool KidStuff,* a children's magazine. She has published articles on varied topics from the arts to nature. She currently edits and designs a newsletter for the state parks of northwest Florida. As a freelance computer graphic and desktop publishing specialist she designs brochure and page layouts. She edited and wrote the text for *Dean Mitchell: The Early Years*, a profile of the American realist painter. As marketing manager of the quality-of-life division of a navy base, Ms. Ake publicizes and produces publications for the installation's leisure and recreational activities.